Toward
Social Sanity
and
Human Survival

Trigant Burrow

Toward
Social Sanity
and
Human Survival

SELECTIONS FROM HIS WRITINGS EDITED BY
ALFREDA S. GALT

INTRODUCTION BY
STANLEY BURNSHAW

HORIZON PRESS   NEW YORK

Copyright © 1984 by The Lifwynn Foundation

Library of Congress Cataloging in Publication Data

Burrow, Trigant, 1875–1950.
  Trigant Burrow, toward social sanity and human
survival.

  Bibliography: p.
  Includes index.
  1. Consciousness—Addresses, essays, lectures.
2. Social psychology—Addresses, essays, lectures.
3. Group psychoanalysis—Addresses, essays, lectures.
4. Self—Addresses, essays, lectures.   I. Galt, Alfreda S.
II. Title. III. Title: Toward social sanity and human
survival.
BF311.B853   1984   150.19′5   82-48440
ISBN 0-8180-1450-4

Manufactured in the United States of America

Contents

Introduction by Stanley Burnshaw   *vii*

Foreword by Alfreda S. Galt   *xv*

Preface by Trigant Burrow   *xxxv*

Chapter
  I   The Solidarity of the Species   *1*
 II   Phyloanalysis: A Study of the Social Self   *25*
III   Origins of a Social Neurosis   *53*
 IV   The "How" of Attention   *79*
  V   Working with Tensions   *107*
 VI   The Global Whole   *133*

Glossary   *151*
Acknowledgments   *155*
Bibliography   *157*
Index   *167*

Introduction

STANLEY BURNSHAW

It was just four decades ago that I first "encountered" Trigant Burrow—through the aid of a book by a friend, Herbert J. Muller. The discussion of "problems and premises" in his newly published *Science and Criticism*[1] made me impatient for more, and the opening pages on "the implications of modern science" lived up to the author's intent: "to make," as he phrased it, "really available, for the purposes of literary criticism, the revolutionary findings in the natural and social sciences." No work could have seemed more pertinent to my purposes for, at the time, after years of reviewing books and plays, I was striving to master the final version of what, in a drastically different form, would much later (1970) appear as *The Seamless Web*. No one, I felt, but Muller possessed the discernment, knowledge, the calm and the wit "to work out some implications of some of the more significant developments" marking these fields of study. I had come to esteem his abilities in the course of my year at Cornell,

---

[1] Yale Univ. Press, 1943. Herbert J. Muller (1905–1980), still at times confused with his late cousin Hermann J. Muller, the Nobel laureate in Physics and Medicine for 1946, earned almost instant acclaim with *The Uses of the Past* (1952), his study of history's meaning and values.

where he lectured on literature. I had also learned how to listen whenever he damned or praised or singled out something—an author, a work—as calling for thoughtful attention. Hence, when I read his opening page on "Social Biology," I knew I had touched something crucial.

Muller had already dealt with biology's shift from a mechanistic approach to a view of the organism as a whole: the time had come for him to widen the range by including the group. Ready to hand was the well-known study of social insects by W. M. Wheeler, who maintained that an ant colony is not a conceptual fiction but a true organism:

> In such implications of the organismic concepts [Muller goes on], biology approaches sociology. Meanwhile it has supplied the basis for at least one revolutionary social theory—the theory detonated by Trigant Burrow in *The Biology of Human Conflict* [1937]. Few thinkers appear to have noticed the explosion; but if Dr. Burrow is right, he has shattered the foundations of almost all the world's thought.

To which one must say "Not quite"—as Muller himself concedes in his pages that follow. They attempt to make clear a number of concepts central to Burrow's beliefs, citing such matters as false *vs.* valid means for observing objectively (by including one's self in the group); the effort through "phyloanalysis"[2] to get to the bases of biological behavior as well as social conduct, and so to define the *inherently* normal; the enor-

---

[2] Burrow discarded the term "group analysis" in favor of "phyloanalysis" because the "group" never meant for him a conventionally assembled collection of individuals. He had in mind a biological group and a biological principle of behavior—as he put it, "because of this organismic principle of behavior underlying our researches." (*The Neurosis of Man*, pp. 91f.)

mous gap existing between our intrinsic feelings and the social expression we give them; and the deep disharmony between the primary, total organismic processes and the secondary, partial system of responses to word-signs, resulting (to quote Burrow) in verbal "symbols that *represent* conduct" rather than the "biological processes that *are* conduct." There is virtually nothing concerning Burrow's first salvo, *The Social Basis of Consciousness* (1927). Understandably so—for, as Muller feels forced to point out, one "embarrassment" of Burrow's "alarming" theory is that it wholly "disarms criticism"; and critics—Muller is one of them—"perforce depend on the symbolic processes [that is], on mere words and ideas." And yet at the end he commends Burrow for attacking the "real abuses of intellect and dangers of symbols; we unquestionably do suffer from an imbalance."

For a writer profoundly tied to conventional views of mentation Muller's report is surprisingly fair—with one large exception: his treatment of Burrow's idea of the "preconscious" state and its meaning for human behavior. Here one does better to turn to D. H. Lawrence and his long, sympathetic review of *The Social Basis of Consciousness*.[3] Muller does not, however, quote from Burrow's own account of the birth of phyloanalysis in 1918:

> Having years ago been "analyzed" in preparation for my work in psychopathology, I had been for years duly "analyzing" others. It unexpectedly happened one day, however, that while I was interpreting a dream of a student-assistant, he made bold to challenge the honesty of my analytic position, insisting that . . . the test of

---

[3] *The Bookman*, New York, November, 1927, "A New Theory of Neuroses," pp. 314 ff.

my sincerity would be met only when I should myself
be willing to accept from him the same analytic exactions I was now imposing on others. . . . [S]uch a proposition seemed to me nothing short of absurd. Had I
not been "analyzed"? Needless to say I had heard this
proposal from patients many times before, but while
my reaction to the suggestion in the present instance
was chiefly one of amusement, my pride was not a little piqued at the intimation it conveyed. So with the
thought that in the interest of experiment it could at
least do no harm to humor for a time the waywardness
of inexperience, I conceded the arrangement.

Not many weeks after I had taken the patient's chair
and yielded him mine I realized that . . . "my resistances" to my self-appointed analyst, far from being
negligible, were plainly insuperable . . . . What calls for
more vital emphasis, however, is the fact that . . . there
came gradually to me the realization that my analyst, in
changing places with me, had merely shifted to the authoritarian vantage-ground I had myself relinquished
and that the situation had remained essentially unaltered still. . . . It marked at once the opening of wholly
new vistas of experience.[4]

What followed has now become history: the development and continuing refinement of a method of
group analysis which was formally started with his
group analytic studies at Lifwynn Camp in the summer of 1923, then carried forward with the establishment of The Lifwynn Foundation. Decades would
pass before his fellow-professionals would begin to
perceive the trail-blazing nature and meaningfulness
of his work. Burrow's writings—provocative, piercing,
and shocking—were quietly shelved. He lost his university ties; was in effect evicted (1932) from the

---

[4] For Burrow's full statement, see his Preface in this book.

American Psychoanalytic Association of which he had been a founder and one-time President; and for all practical purposes, a taboo was placed on his name.

Four of the twelve scientific reviews of his first volume, *The Social Basis of Consciousness* (1927) were fairly favorable, however, and six respectful but critical. *The Biology of Human Conflict* (1937) evoked a curious shift: ten professional reviews proved positive, ten respectful, nine negative. But a marked change for the worse occurred when the volume he viewed as his *magnum opus, The Neurosis of Man,* appeared (1949). Nine years later, however, the tone of response to his posthumous letters, *A Search for Man's Sanity,* was surprisingly positive. Finally, with *Preconscious Foundations of Human Experience* in 1964 the reversal arrived. Trigant Burrow's concepts "represent now, in essence, the vanguard of a new social-psychiatric approach to mental health, the core of an advancing science of human behavior," wrote Dr. Nathan W. Ackerman in his Foreword. "One by one," he continued, "Burrow's concepts begin to re-emerge in the current literature, but, oddly enough, not as coming from him. Piecemeal, they reappear and gain strength" in the writing of latterday scholars. And not only is Burrow "in many ways to be regarded [now] as the outstanding pioneer in the whole science of the study of small groups" (wrote Eric Berne), "Trigant Burrow was certainly fifty to one hundred years ahead of his time" (Cornelius Beukenkamp).[5]

Such belated tributes, fine though they are, somehow fall short of the mark. More to the point is the

---

[5] Berne: *The Structure and Dynamics of Organizations and Groups,* Lippincott, 1963, pp. 215 ff.; Beukenkamp: *International Journal of Group Psychotherapy,* New York, XV, July, 1965.

view and response of a man of letters who was also "a man of all thought": Sir Herbert Read, for whom Burrow, more than anyone else, had "explained the secret of cultural vitality" while proposing as well "the new foundations" for the oncoming phase of the evolution of man.[6] Nine years after this declaration, Read wrote a Foreword to *A Search for Man's Sanity*, the volume of Burrow's selected letters, replete with biographical notes and a strikingly useful index. The book, as Sir Herbert observes, "by revealing the man, explains his work," which in many respects it does. And yet the reader—layman or scientist—needs to complement this personal record with the essay by Dr. Hans Syz on "Phylopathology"[7] and of course with the present volume. Though Dr. Syz's essay may not be easy to find, the effort involved will be well worthwhile, for no clearer summary statement of Burrow's achievement has as yet been made. It also provides for the reader who plans to explore *Preconscious Foundations of Human Experience* (1964)[8] the background of thought and experimentation out of which the whole of Burrow's contribution emerged.

It is difficult for me to write only briefly about that work. I have already tried to express in *The Seamless Web* my sense of its supreme significance for the story of man on earth and the "science" of man. Moreover, that "the preconscious mode" and all it involves were

---

[6] *The Tiger's Eye*, New York, October 1949, pp. 115–17.

[7] *Encyclopedia of Psychology* edited by Philip L. Harriman, Philosophical Library, New York, 1946, pp. 519–523.

[8] Burrow: *Preconscious Foundations of Human Experience*. New York: Basic Books, 1964, pp. xxxv, 164. Burrow's term "preconscious" must be differentiated from the psychoanalytic designation "preconscious" or "foreconscious," which means simply the aspect of mind that borders on consciousness.

the "favorite theme" of Burrow; that it proved, as it were, the source of which his subsequent work was the "fuller expression," struck me as no surprise when I found these statements in his later letters. It could not, I felt, have been otherwise in the life of a man who had early found his way to this "strifeless phase of human awareness" and its implications. Hence, rather than offer again the pages I wrote on the relevance of Burrow's work to human divisiveness, let me urge readers to turn to the Foreword by Nathan W. Ackerman to *Preconscious Foundations of Human Experience.*

They will gain much more than a helpful orientation to the "final words" of Burrow on preconscious foundations. In the course of his wide-ranging pages, Dr. Ackerman offers a strikingly fresh perspective on both the work and career of Burrow, bringing into view some relationships which had not hitherto been perceived. Of especial aid to initiates is his summary sketch of Burrow's "main contributions," of their modes of difference from Freud's, of their kinship to Walter B. Cannon's.

Toward the end of his essay, Ackerman faces the reader with the ultimate human problem. "What do we mean," he asks, "when we exclaim with horror that our world is going mad?" "And who is sick—the individual, the family, society?" We must, he warns, re-think this entire question. Meanwhile "Steadily the evidence mounts in biology, ethology, social psychology, anthropology, and psychiatry to substantiate Burrow's main thesis of a primary biosocial union"—"Evidence," moreover, "accumulates in the field of biology and the science of human relations to support the importance of a basic current of social interdependence and cooperation throughout animal forms." In the light of such facts as these, he avers, "Burrow's theory rests on firm biological grounds." It is more than a fitting conclusion. It is also a fitting tribute to one "who had struggled throughout his entire life to understand the worst of all plagues—man against man."

I know of no better introduction to Burrow's achievement than the present work, so ably and comprehensively edited by Alfreda S. Galt, who is uniquely qualified for this timely task.

Martha's Vineyard, May 1983   —S. B.

Foreword

ALFREDA S. GALT

In his distinguished Introduction Stanley Burnshaw mentions Herbert Read's 1949 review of Burrow's *The Neurosis of Man*. In it, Read wrote, "Somewhere and somehow, round about 1927, D. H. Lawrence communicated to me his enthusiasm for a new psychologist, Trigant Burrow. . . . From that time, more than twenty years ago, I have never been able to understand why, in his own country, ⌊Burrow⌋ has not received the recognition due to one of the greatest psychologists of our time. It seems to me that only Freud and Jung come into comparison with him, and in certain respects Trigant Burrow is, as Lawrence said in his review [of Burrow's first book]* deeper and more vital, if less spectacular than Freud.

"What distinguishes Burrow's psychology from the rest, and makes it so important? It is undoubtedly his insistence on the primary importance of the problem of consciousness—of the consciousness that is phylic and socially unified, and the consciousness that is self-regarding and isolating—the self over against other selves. There is nothing particularly original in

---

* Lawrence, D.H., "A New Theory of Neuroses," (review of Burrow, Trigant, *The Social Basis of Consciousness*) *The Bookman*, November, 1927

that distinction as such, but Dr. Burrow treats the
question from a genetic or evolutionary point of view,
and asks what have been the consequences of this
split-consciousness. He finds (and proves by laboratory experiments) that they are not merely mental, but
even physiological (somatic) . . . Only Trigant Burrow
has suggested a *method,* even a technique, by means
of which our social aberrations can be corrected* . . .

Since those words were written, marked changes
have taken place in the study of consciousness and
with them has come increased emphasis on the intrinsic and integral. "The doors of perception" were
opened by psychedelic drugs in the Nineteen-fifties.
There was a great wave of interest in Eastern philosophies with their central theme of cosmic unity. Meditative and somatic techniques became popular; bio-
feedback sharpened awareness of internal dynamics
related to outer behavior. The ecological movement
focused attention on our sense of separation from the
environment, on the need for "planetary consciousness." The human potential movement tried to break
the mold of customary interpersonal relations. And the
science of physics increasingly stressed the bonds that
link each particle in the universe to every other.

It is natural that Burrow, as one of the seminal
thinkers and experimenters of the first half of the cen-
tury, anticipated many of these trends. But it may be
surprising that so much of his work remains fresh and
relevant to the problems of today, and that the frame of
reference from which he addressed them is in many
ways still novel.

Burrow's commitment to a holistic, organismic
view of human consciousness did not develop as an

* *The Tiger's Eye,* October, 1949, pp. 115–17.

abstract, philosophical position. It grew directly out of his observations as a psychoanalyst and it was tested in the grueling group analysis which he later introduced. At the same time his conviction that society-at-large is permeated by a "vast mood contagion" was neither theoretical nor remote. For the accuracy of this diagnosis was evidenced in his own investigation of the interrelational processes of himself and his fellows as elements in a disordered community. He studied *rightness*—the sense of rightness that can set individuals, groups and nations in sullen opposition to one another—as a generic condition common to humanity at large and thus resident within himself and other members of his laboratory group. And he related this phenomenon to a distortion of the sense of self and to underlying somatic processes.

Many more people are sensitive to global problems these days than was the case during Burrow's lifetime. It has seemed as though such people deserve an opportunity to understand his pioneering research, to be able to relate its findings to their own observations, to become acquainted with the procedures and practices of phyloanalysis and to compare them with their own. Does Burrow's investigation have something to add to our understanding of the overwhelming problems that face us today, problems that involve our very survival on this planet? Do his studies provide a further dimension that offers a clue worth pursuing?

This book has been prepared to enable thoughtful readers to answer these questions for themselves, and its unusual form has been dictated by this purpose.

Let us review the highlights of Burrow's career from the beginning of his psychoanalytic practice to his later work as a pioneering social biologist.

II

During their 1909 visit to the United States for the famed Clark lectures, Freud and Jung spent an evening at Hammerstein's Roof Garden in New York. It was there, between acts of the play, that Burrow was introduced to them by A. A. Brill. At that time there was of course no division into Freudian and Jungian "schools" in psychoanalysis—the two men shared a more or less common outlook in this exciting new field. Before the next act of the play began, Burrow had arranged to spend the following winter in Zurich studying with C.G. Jung.

At that point Burrow was working under Adolf Meyer at the New York State Psychiatric Institute on Ward's Island. He had received his medical degree from the University of Virginia. There he had put in a postgraduate year as a demonstrator in biology, followed by a year's work as a clinical assistant abroad.

At Johns Hopkins he had pursued further medical studies and also entered the field of experimental psychology in which he received a doctorate in June 1909. None of these, however, had aroused his enthusiasm as did the study of psychoanalysis.

In spite of his work with Jung and his personal liking for him, Burrow's primary allegiance always remained with Freud. Yet he was a man of independent spirit with a certain uncompromising view that began to assert itself soon after he launched his psychoanalytic practice in Baltimore. Essentially what Burrow saw and began to develop in papers from 1914 on, was that society-at-large embodies the neurotic elements Freud had identified in individual patients. "The policy that leads to the neurotic's self-imposed ostracism differs only in degree from the policy of the community," he wrote in 1914. "For society is hysterical, too. Society has its elaborate system of defense-mechanisms, its equivocations and metonymies, its infantile makeshifts and illusions. The difference is that society's counterfeits possess the advantage of universal currency, and so the record of its frailties is set down under the name of custom rather than of pathology."*

Along with the growing conviction that so-called "normality" represented a shared illness, Burrow began to observe, in certain patients, expressions of a mood that was non-striving, confluent, integrated. It seemed to trace back to the original unity of mother and child in the prenatal and early postnatal phases of development. He formulated the "principle of primary identification" and suggested that this original sense of oneness, rather than Oedipal conflict and competitive desire, underlies and informs the subsequent feeling-life of the individual. Burrow presented this principle of a preconscious mode ("preconscious" meaning the primary phase of consciousness, in contrast to the Freudian usage of the word**) in a series of papers between 1914 and 1917. Oberndorf cites it as one of the outstanding American contributions to psychoanalytic theory before 1920.***

Burrow was a popular analyst and he might have been content to continue his practice indefinitely had it not been for Clarence Shields. As a student-assistant, this young man was undergoing analysis with Burrow

---

* "The Psychanalyst and the Community," p. 6 (Full references will be found in Burrow's bibliography on p. 157)

** For definitions of both usages of *preconscious* see Hinsie and Campbell: *Psychiatric Dictionary, Third Edition;* New York, Oxford University Press, 1960. This term also appears in the Glossary.-Ed.

*** *A History of Psychoanalysis in America,* N.Y.: Grune & Stratton, 1953, p. 237

when he took it upon himself to question the sincerity of his analyst's views. He suggested putting them to the test by reversing their roles, with Shields assuming the position of analyst.

Burrow describes this switch in some detail in the preface to *The Social Basis of Consciousness*. Because this role-reversal constituted the crucial starting point for group analysis and all Burrow's later work, his description is quoted in part by Stanley Burnshaw in his Introduction and is included in full as the Author's Preface immediately following this Foreword. As he makes clear in that statement, the switch in roles, in which Burrow became analysand and Shields analyst, led to an impasse which challenged Burrow's established views on psychoanalysis and the role of the analyst. The "shared sickness" of society, which he had been discussing in theory, came home to the two men as a gross impediment operating within themselves, as well as within the community as a whole. They decided to pursue a mutual analysis but the situation became increasingly strained and eventually they called in others—friends, colleagues, patients—to help them dig into the nature of the interrelational obstruction which they had uncovered. It is significant that the nucleus of this group (which included members of Dr. Burrow's family) remained together as an experimental community for more than thirty years, observing interrelational process as it was revealed in their own interaction. In 1927 The Lifwynn Foundation was established to formalize this laboratory setting for Burrow's unique inquiry.

Burrow was unquestionably a forerunner of group therapies; and, like later group approaches, group analysis focused on the here and now, emphasizing immediate feeling material to the exclusion of the reminiscent or theoretical. It did not, however, constitute Burrow's analysis of the group but rather the group's analysis of the participants including Burrow. And the thrust of the investigation was not "adjustment" of the individual but analysis of the social neurosis as exemplified in the group and its various members and clusters.

The titles of papers emerging from this experiment indicate the broad nature of the study: "Social Images versus Reality" (1924), "A Relative Concept of Consciousness" (1925), "The Laboratory Method in Psychoanalysis," "Our Mass Neurosis," "Insanity a Social Problem," all in 1926. They stressed a general mood distortion, an overemphasis on false "social images" that vicariously rule our relationships, and especially an accentuation of the image of the self as a discrete entity, separate and discontinuous from other selves.

By this time Burrow had come to regard psychoanalysis, as practiced by his fellow analysts (and formerly by himself), as protecting the status quo of "normality," the "reaction-average" which, in spite of its prevalence, did not represent a norm of community health. At meeting after meeting of the American Psychoanalytic Association (of which he was a founder in 1911 and president in 1926), he presented his method and tried to involve other members in his approach. But his colleagues there and in the other associations he addressed were unresponsive to his frequent indictments of their field. Possibly the coolness that developed toward him in those early days contributed to the later neglect of Burrow's work which developed in this country. Certainly Burrow did not endear himself

to his colleagues with such statements as "In its present unconscious social involvement, psychoanalysis is
not the study of a neurosis; it *is* a neurosis. It is not an
objective science applied to a subjective disease; it is a
subjective reflection of the very disease it presumably
submits to objective scientific study."*

III

The underlying physiology of consciousness was
always important to Burrow. In a 1913 paper, "The
Meaning of the Psychic Factor," he suggested a modification and extension of the James-Lange theory.
Recognizing that the "psychic" and the "physiological" are but two sides of a single coin, he writes,
"There is no longer any such thing as 'mental' in the
older dualistic sense. Such conceptions belong to the
dark ages . . . Surely it is time for the physician to recast
his ideas in respect to the biological data of mind and
to realize that mind is somatic."**

However, from 1927 on, Burrow's concern with
the physiological and organic took on expanded meaning in his papers. "As the human body is more than the
sum of the elements composing it, so the social body is
more than the sum of its elements . . . The physiological synthesis which interrelates the several elements
composing the group . . . unites them into a functioning whole . . . Processes that are inter-functional [be-
tween organisms] are not less physiological than processes that are restricted within the circumscribed
organism of the single individual."

But to study the physiology that unites the ele-

---

* "The Problem of the Transference," p. 201
** "The Meaning of the Psychic Factor," p. 10

ments of a group or species, "it is required that the observer 'correct for' his own subjective behavior, personally and socially and so render objectively observable the physiological behavior of those social groups of which he himself is an integral, physiological part."*

Such statements grew naturally out of the experience of the laboratory group. For as the common social expressions, the "normal" give-and-take of interrelational life, were more and more called into question, the closer the participants came to sensing the tensions and internal strains associated with such give-and-take. They came to experience certain physiological sensations which seemed to be related to interferences in communication. Burrow defined these tensions in terms of a lag or deflection in the process of attention, the physiological function that mediates between organism and environment.

In *The Structure of Insanity* (1932) Burrow presented his observations about a possible conflict between two kinds of attention. One, the deflected mode he later called *ditention,* appeared to characterize "normal" adaptation generally. In the ditentive mode of relating to the physical and social environment, attention becomes tied up with the image of the self and fails to make direct contact with its surroundings. This lag permits behavior that is inappropriate or destructive, from the viewpoint of the organism as a whole, to pass as acceptable or even "healthy."

Cotention, on the other hand, was found to be an inclusive, immediate way of attending. Burrow described it as the species' basic attentional mode, em-

* "The Physiological Basis of Neurosis and Dream," p. 49, p. 56

bodying the tensional integration of the race and its balanced interrelational function. Against the background of cotention it was possible to sense the "unnatural" strains and tensions of ditention and their interference with the social functioning of human beings. Development of the capacity to discriminate between cotention and ditention became a major focus of the research and led to instrumental studies of changes in respiration, brainwaves and eye-movements as subjects shifted from ditention to cotention. At the same time Burrow and his associates were deeply involved in observing the effects of the cotentive mode on interrelational process within themselves as an experimental community. For it was their belief that, by defining a conflict in patterns of neuromuscular tension, they provided a clue to the biophysical nature of human relational disorder, whether such disorder is expressed between people, between nations or between the species and its environment.

IV

As a teen-ager, I took part in one of the early group sessions and it may be that my memories, as a student of Burrow's, will serve to illustrate certain aspects of his research. My mother had become interested in this novel study and I accompanied her in 1926 to Lifwynn Camp in the Adirondacks. This was the Burrows' summer place, which, with the inception of group analysis, had become the setting for concentrated summer study. Beautiful, rustic and accessible only by boat, the camp was an ideal setting for mutual observation of group interaction.

The study at that time was still in an early phase. There were twenty-four participants, aged 15 to 55

and, with the exception of youngsters like myself, most
had had previous exposure to Burrow's investigation. We shared the camp work (cooking, marketing,
groundswork, etc.) and at least a nominal commitment
to the research aim. This research aim was to observe
and report covert motivations in the immediate moment in the individual (oneself or another) and in the
group.

To further this purpose, there were, in this early
stage, regularly scheduled meetings of the group as a
whole, as well as of smaller units. And every meal was
regarded as a laboratory session where the group
might consider its own interrelational dilemmas. Finally, members were expected to interrupt ongoing activities at any time to focus on underlying motivations.

Shortly after our arrival, a general meeting was
held when orientation talks were given by Dr. Burrow
and others. As the meeting broke up, one of the new-
comers found she had left her flashlight at her cabin,
some distance away through the woods. At once a vet-
eran of previous summers offered hers. "Take mine,"
she said with a warm smile. From the end of the room
Burrow interrupted our preparations to leave. This
brief exchange, he explained, illustrated one kind of
situation he hoped we would be looking at during the
next two months: What was the occasion of the over-
sight? What prompted the offer of help? Was there a
sound way to determine need that did not depend on
our usual evaluations?

Certain amenities—for instance, the habit of
greeting each other as we met for breakfast—were dis-
pensed with for experimental purposes during the
summer. This omission was not because Burrow did
not value good manners under ordinary circumstances

—his own were impeccable. But circumstances at the camp were not ordinary, and it was instructive to discover how much we depend upon such daily rituals as greeting. This in turn brought into focus our dependence upon the signals of geniality, and the underlying insecurity of the group mood.

During the summer, evidence accumulated for the students that their own immediate interrelational reactions were almost always self-defensive or self-aggrandizing, no matter how these reactions were expressed. This insight did not come with a sudden, stunning clarity. It was an elusive observation, easily overlooked or denied. But the possessiveness of love, the "I'll scratch your back; you scratch mine" attitude in interrelational life, the presence of secret competitiveness, etc., came painfully to awareness again and again. In T-groups and encounter groups which developed many years later and in some of which I took part, I did not find anything comparable to this examination of self.

On the other hand, in the Sixties and Seventies, it seemed easier for people in such groups to accept the condition of remaining in the here and now. To those of us who were attempting it for the first time in 1926, it was difficult and uncomfortable. Nothing we had done previously prepared us for it. The tendency to bring up reminiscent material, to theorize, to say what one felt expected to say, often took precedence over simple observation. Moreover, the outside community did not provide the same understanding of group endeavor that we are accustomed to today. For instance, on my return from Lifwynn Camp, I tried to explain to schoolmates "how I spent my summer vacation" and found them totally uncomprehending.

Under the circumstances it was inevitable that Dr. Burrow, and to a lesser degree his co-worker, Clarence Shields, should have occupied the position of leaders. They had submitted themselves to a mutual analysis and it was out of their need for a wider setting that the laboratory group came into being. Naturally, they seemed to be parental figures—or did they? When the group analytic approach was brought to bear on the leader/led situation as a whole, a new dimension was added. The common elements in the two positions became evident and could be examined from the broad premises of the research. But this development occurred in only a limited way during that early summer. Later, as the work with physiological tensions advanced, students had a tangible background from which to make such observations.

The camp continued to be used as the Summer Research Station of The Lifwynn Foundation from the time the organization was established in 1927. It was several years, however, before I visited there again and a long time before I returned as a serious student. By then, the early phase I had known with its greater emphasis on verbal analysis, had evolved into the work with internal tensional patterns. To me the mood seemed calmer, more mellow, and the cordiality to a young visitor was marked.

The group was smaller at that point, consisting of the dozen or so individuals who formed the core of The Lifwynn Foundation and included the professional associates who had worked with Burrow and Shields from the start. There were also visitors and helpers (the campers no longer attempted all the work) and, as time went on, the children and grandchildren of group members. I might add that the predominance of continuing real-life relationships within the group—sisters, colleagues, parents and children, husbands and wives—remains unique in my experience with group work.

Some of the preliminary work with instrumental recordings was done at the camp and Burrow also did much of his writing there, often with a group of co-workers. I do not recall meetings in later years specifically arranged for the study of interrelational reactions. In earlier days, subtle or overt expressions of irritation, infatuation, nostalgia, dependence, etc., often occupied the group meetings. But from the mid-Thirties the work focused on discrimination of the contrasting patterns of internal tension that Burrow had identified. Such experimentation could be carried out at any time, and every meal offered opportunities for the student to report to the group on the ways this internal observation affected perception and behavior. Burrow made no attempt to impose a mass shift to the basic attentive mode. Rather the dining (that is, the laboratory) table was seen as an arena where a complex combination of biological needs and social conditioning was expressed. Mealtimes, in other words, provided a situation in which students could gain a group perspective on their own involvement in the disorder of society, as this disorder overlies and distorts coordinated interrelational function.

Burrow, in my recollection, was a man of charm and wit, with a sense of fun that seemed ready to bubble up at almost any moment. A true physician, he was deeply interested in the people around him, whether they were co-workers, family members, cab drivers or people he met on a train. I often saw him put his work aside to give full attention to someone's personal prob-

lems. On the other hand, he could appear harsh in following up his observations of the social neurosis—he
felt he shared it with other members of the laboratory
and was wholly committed to the task of investigating
it. Hence he did not spare the "feelings" of the student
or students who seemed at the moment to exemplify
the trend to disorder. In fact, from working with his
own reactions, he found that such feelings were themselves distorted and that freedom came only through a
radical shift of internal perspective or attention.

Clarence Shields occasionally remarked that Dr.
Burrow could have been a "great man" if he had
wanted to be. He had the charisma and dedication to
have led a "movement" but he did not consider himself a guru or reformer. More than once he was urged
to popularize his work and to build up a wider public
for it, but he always demurred.* As a laboratory investigator, he felt obliged to present his fellow scientists
with the evidence as he saw it. It was his hope that
they would follow up on his findings and test them for
themselves.

V

I have spoken of the timeliness of much of Burrow's writing. This applies to two areas which have
been prominent recently in public discussion. First,
with regard to the position of women, Burrow was
keenly aware of its artificiality and of its repressive nature. He speaks of a trend "which in the woman has
led to the adoption of the role corresponding to the
mental image female and in the man to the *mental*

---

* For instance, see *A Search for Man's Sanity, The Selected Letters of
Trigant Burrow,* p. 444

image male ... It makes it obligatory upon the woman
that she repress the male element within her notwithstanding that it is a no less constituent factor than the
female element in composing the bipolar quality essential to the unity of her organism."* This may
suggest Jung's formulation of anima/animus. However, Burrow relates the suppression of this underlying androgyny to a pervasive "ego-sexuality"** which
in his view has come to dominate our organic sex instinct, just as the divisive self-image has come to dis-
tort other areas of human interchange.

In another area, Burrow's confidence in the ultimate effectiveness of science to solve the problems of
our species is evident throughout his writings. He believed that "what the child has by nature and the scientist by training, all mankind possesses potentially in
the primary unity and integrity of his total organism's
relation to its environment."*** His entire life's work
was an effort to apply the principles of science to the
subjective life of the human animal.

Yet Burrow had a healthy skepticism regarding
scientists and their motivations and would have felt no
surprise at some of the technological and environmental nightmares which have become familiar to us in recent years. "It is highly expedient that the scientific
mind bring itself to take account of the unscientific
mood within itself," he wrote in *The Neurosis of Man*
(p. 200).

Burrow regarded conflict, alienation, crime and
war as problems in public health to be solved by the

---

* *The Social Basis of Consciousness*, pp. 216–17.
** Ibid., p. 203
*** "Prescription for Peace," p. 110

scientific method. While his writing sometimes soars in a kind of poetic expression, it is for the most part prosaic and factual. Perhaps this very quality may be welcome to researchers who find that their observations about the intrinsic interconnectedness of the species tend to parallel Burrow's. They will find in him an ally in the Western scientific tradition, one who believes that science is capable of identifying and neutralizing those feelings and sensations which interfere with our natural harmony and coordination.

VI

As editor, I have taken some liberties with Burrow's material. Like the views of other outstanding men of his time—Korzybski, Goldstein, von Bertalanffy, for example—many of Burrow's ideas are represented in the current culture and no longer have their original impact. This includes some of his comments on Freudian interpretations, his insistence on inclusion of the analyst in the total situation, some of his references to the inconsistencies and inadequacies of the so-called "normal" adjustment, and his questioning of the dichotomy popularly drawn between "normal" and "neurotic." I have included few selections on such subjects in order to free the reader to focus on material that appears to me of special relevance at the present time. Perhaps the greatest liberty I have taken has been to go directly, in Chapter I, to the positive, central core of Burrow's researches—his formulation of the principle of species solidarity, the tensional rapport that exists throughout the phylum as an expression of its biological heritage.

Burrow himself led carefully through slow stages up to the presentation of this species/organismic frame of reference. But readers of today are perhaps in a better position than those of Burrow's time to consider the significance of this broad framework in the light of recent studies. It is at any rate the starting point I have selected for this book, followed in subsequent chapters by Burrow's descriptions of his methodology, theory, procedures and instrumental studies, and his views on the future development of his work.

To present this wealth of material, I have chosen short excerpts from the range of Burrow's writings. But the passages are not meant to be read separately or at random; they follow each other in a logical sequence and present a rounded statement of his thesis. I have made virtually no changes in Burrow's original expression with the exception of adding a few such blending words as "however," "therefore," or "thus." But I have permitted myself to make whatever cuts appeared helpful in clarifying or highlighting the central idea of a passage. I hope that admirers of Burrow who are familiar with his writings will forgive me for taking this liberty and for failing to indicate by elision dots where cuts have been made. It seemed to me that such indications would be distracting in following the flow of the discourse.

The majority of the excerpts are drawn from Burrow's later writings, particularly his book, *The Neurosis of Man,* and the papers, "Prescription for Peace" and "Emotion and the Social Crisis." The date at the end of each selection indicates when it was written and detailed references are given in the source notes at the close of each chapter. A list of Burrow's published writings with complete references appears on page 157. Acknowledgements appear on page 155.

A glossary of special terms on page 151 includes

definitions of new words originated by Burrow and special usages he developed for words in general use. In addition, chapter notes and footnotes alert the reader to some of Burrow's words as they are introduced. Footnotes, unless otherwise indicated, are part of the original text.

It would be misleading to give the impression that this book embodies the sweep of Burrow's total thesis—many aspects, most notably his neurological theories, are only hinted at. But if my selection does nothing more than encourage readers to turn to Burrow's full works, it will have been worth the time spent on its preparation. His thesis is remarkably compact and consistent and I may have been overly bold in thinking it could be encompassed in the form which I have chosen. So whatever its faults, I hope they will be placed at the door of the editor and that readers who find the excerpts stimulating will turn to the original sources for the original substance. Judging by the depth of my own response to the work of Trigant Burrow they will find it a rewarding journey.

VII

The writings that make up this book are products of a unique group experiment and it is appropriate that I should have had the assistance of a farflung group in preparing it. Most of the members are not known to one another but they have shared a common appreciation of Trigant Burrow's research. Among them are Theodore F. Beimler, the late Kingsley H. Birge, Sidney M. Guimarães, Ralph Hurttlen, and Russell H. Miles. Their comments on the manuscript, sometimes critical but always sympathetic to its purpose, have enhanced the final product.

Michele Frome and Elizabeth Galt were especially helpful in relation to editorial precision and clarification of content. I am also indebted to John Wikse for his thoughtful evaluation and to Montague Ullman and Michael Sperber for their encouragement and help. Dr. Ullman's discerning insights and suggestions were most valuable; and Dr. Sperber's considerate review of the manuscript and recommendations for it contributed tellingly, particularly to the Editor's Notes. He also suggested our title.

Hans Syz, M.D., president of The Lifwynn Foundation, has been in touch with the book since its inception, and I value deeply the unfailing concern he has had for its development. The project has indeed benefited from his keen discrimination and penetrating critique. Stanley Burnshaw's immediate and warmhearted sympathy for the aims of this endeavor has been a source of encouragement and I am profoundly grateful for his stimulating Introduction and for his comprehensive and enlightened comments on the significance of Burrow's contributions. Nor can I close my acknowledgments without a word of appreciation for Ben Raeburn's consummate editorial skill and the wisdom of his counsel.

Thanks go also to Maureen Cotter and Penny White for their care and consideration in preparing the manuscript for publication.

April, 1983 —A.S.G.

Preface

TRIGANT BURROW*

I do not know whether I can make clear in what manner the conception embodied in the following pages first arose. Conceptions derived from data of reason and observation necessarily proceed from a mental basis. Scientific and philosophical treatises are the outcome primarily of scientific or philosophical ideas. With both inductive and deductive methods of reasoning the conclusions that flow from the assumptions are our accepted basis of procedure. With the method of the present study, however, we are upon other ground, for the inception of this work was in no such wise; and yet to say that it is based upon no conceptual premise would, of course, not be true. The difference is that what follows here has been the outgrowth of events that were prior to and independent of any conceptual formulation of them. Biological necessity preceded and argument followed after. My meaning may for the moment be best understood when it is considered that these events are the processes of per-

---

* Preface to Burrow's first book, *The Social Basis of Consciousness*, pp. xv–xviii

sonal experience inseparable from the sequences here embodied. While this is not the place for detailing personal history, the presentation of a thesis as intimate as this would not be complete without some concrete account of its origin.

Having years ago been "analyzed" in preparation for my work in psychopathology, I had been for years duly "analyzing" others. It unexpectedly happened one day, however, that while I was interpreting a dream of a student-assistant, he made bold to challenge the honesty of my analytic position, insisting that, as far as he was concerned, the test of my sincerity would be met only when I should myself be willing to accept from him the same analytic exactions I was now imposing upon others. As may be readily judged, such a proposition seemed to me nothing short of absurd. Had I not been "analyzed"? Needless to say I had heard this proposal from patients many times before, but while my reaction to the suggestion in the present instance was chiefly one of amusement, my pride was not a little piqued at the intimation it conveyed. So with the thought that in the interest of experiment it could at least do no harm to humor for a time the waywardness of inexperience, I conceded the arrangement.

Not many weeks after I had taken the patient's chair and yielded him mine I realized that a situation to which I had agreed with more or less levity had assumed an aspect of the profoundest seriousness. My "resistances" to my self-appointed analyst, far from being negligible, were plainly insuperable, but there was now no turning back. The analysis proceeded on its course from day to day and with it my resistances took tighter hold upon me. The agreement to which I had voluntarily lent myself was becoming painful beyond words. Whatever empirical interest the situation may have held for me at the outset was now wholly subordinated to the indignation and pain of the position to which I had been brought.

It is possible to indicate only in their broadest lines the progressive events of these trying months. I need hardly record the growing sense of self-limitation and defeat that went hand in hand with this daily advancing personal challenge, nor the corresponding efforts of concealment in unconscious symbolizations and distortions on my part. What calls for more vital emphasis, however, is the fact that along with the deepening, if reluctant, realization of my intolerance of self-defeat, there came gradually to me the realization that my analyst, in changing places with me, had merely shifted to the authoritarian vantage-ground I had myself relinquished and that the situation had remained essentially unaltered still.

This was significant. It marked at once the opening of wholly new vistas of experience. In the light of its discovery I began to sense for the first time what had all along underlain my own analysis and what, as I now see it, really underlies every analysis. I began to see that the student before me, notwithstanding his undoubted sincerity of purpose, presented a no less personal and proprietary attitude toward me than I had held toward him and that all that had been needed was the authoritarian background to bring this attitude to expression. With the consciousness of this condition I saw what has been for me the crucial revelation of the many years of my analytic work—that, in its individualistic application, the attitude of the psychoanalyst and the attitude of the authoritarian are inseparable.

As from day to day this realization came more closely home to me, and with it the growing acceptance of the limitation and one-sidedness of the personalistic critique in psychoanalysis, my personal self-vindication and resistances began in the same measure to abate. At the same time the analyst too, Mr. Clarence Shields, came at last into a position to sense the personalism and resistance that had unconsciously all along actuated his own reaction. From now forward the direction of the inquiry was completely altered. The analysis henceforth consisted in the reciprocal effort of each of us to recognize within himself his attitude of authoritarianism and autocracy toward the other. With this automatic relinquishment of the personalistic or private basis and its replacement by a more inclusive attitude toward the problems of human consciousness, there has been not alone for myself but also for students and patients a gradual clearing of our entire analytic horizon.

It will later become clearer how this newer formulation of psychoanalysis on the wider basis of its more inclusive impersonal meaning has occurred entirely apart from the common processes of logic. Only the accidental circumstance of a student's protest against my own personal bias, and my subsequent observation of an identical personalism in himself, as empirically disclosed upon our interchanging places, are answerable for the altered insight into psychoanalysis that the recent years have afforded me—an insight which the investigations of the small group of students working along analytic lines identical with my own have more and more substantiated. It was due, then, entirely to this unexpected turn of the tables, which placed me in the role of the patient and the patient in the analytic role, that I was fortuitously launched into my years of social experimentation upon the discrepancies of an individualistic analysis. If the outcome of the process has been the retraction of my earlier analytic outlook, it has not been the expression of any personal acumen or distinctive asset on my part.

The chance eventuality I have mentioned is alone responsible for enforcing the relinquishment of my habitual personalistic basis in psychoanalysis and bringing me to feel the need of a more comprehensive interpretation of the unconscious. Coming to sense, through a wider recognition of the unconscious, the correspondingly larger meaning of the consciousness of man, I have come to feel the need of its more adequate interpretation in such an organismic view as I have attempted to outline under the theme of *The Social Basis of Consciousness*.

—T.B.

I

The Solidarity of the Species

Editor's Note

The selections in this chapter, drawn from writings published between 1925 and 1950, reflect Burrow's experience of an organic continuity uniting the elements of the race. This generic frame of reference characterized his studies throughout. It was both a premise for his group analytic inquiry and a finding of that research. For the "solidarity of the species," intimated in his earliest writings, came to active awareness through the probing of group analysis.

This chapter also considers impediments that interfere with the expression of basic capacities for interrelational health. Burrow believed that in the course of social evolution our primary unity was inadvertently distorted, and that we have substituted an arbitrary standard called "normality." Our maladaptation is now so extensively systematized that a social neurosis exists throughout the species.

Burrow did not see the individual as opposed to society but rather as the embodiment of it. Society's ills and dislocations, as well as its underlying solidarity and strength, are present in all elements of the species—in individuals, groups, and nations. And the endless variety, originality, and creativity of human

1

beings springs from the boundless capacities of the race.

In reports on his research, Burrow found himself handicapped by a lack of precise terms—for example, there were no words that carried the connotation of humanity as an organism. So he borrowed from ancient Greek the word phylum, *meaning "race" or "tribe" and combined it with other words to describe his studies:* phyloanalysis, phylobiology, phylopathology, *etc. Some of these terms appear in Chapter I, among them* phyloorganism *which signifies the human species as a vast interlinked whole.*

In the decades to come, there will undoubtedly be an increasing focus on consciousness and ways to expand our current mode of awareness. Burrow's finding that an "organic principle of consciousness" (p. 6) is active in humankind, in spite of manifold symptoms of conflict and division, can provide an important insight for such studies.

It would seem that there are bonds—innate, intrinsic bonds of purpose and effectiveness—which give consistency and solidarity to the organism of the individual, as they give consistency and solidarity to the organism that comprises the species of man as a race. This solidarity of purpose—this integrative urge within the processes of man—is represented organically in an undercurrent of function that is continuous throughout the organs and tissues of the body. This physiological undercurrent of function with its consistency of purpose extending throughout the organism is a condition with which man has lost touch. His preoccupations with the separate, discrete elements that constitute his personal and conventional interests have tended to replace and to deprive him of a sense of this deeper biological endowment. In our constant entertainment with the symbols of life we have become less and less at home with life itself. (1937)[1]

Thought is synonomous with communication or speech. "They say," "people tell me," "get this," "have you heard?"—such phrases are repeated on every hand and attest our interest in communication through thought. But these current modes of address betoken only a superficial, symbolic form of interchange. In this book we shall attempt to reach, or rather recover, a level of understanding and communication that is more fundamental. We shall try to attain a deeper level of contact and articulation. We shall be interested not so much in acquired forms of verbal thought and interchange as in an internal communication among people based upon the continuity that primarily knits them into a common and unitary race or species. In our phylobiological researches we were not concerned with what the intellectualized and sophisticated individual thinks about the genus man but with what the genus man thinks about the intellectualized and sophisticated individual. It was the avowed purpose of our investigations to discover and, if possible, restore those biological principles of behavior that are intrinsic to us and that insure man's basic relation to the external universe and to his kind. (1949)[2]

As our procedure deals with the reactions of human beings in their personal and social relationships as experienced also by ourselves, we shall be assisted if, preliminary to our inquiry, we shall recall certain biological considerations first brought to the attention of science through the investigations of Darwin. I have in mind the observations of Darwin respecting the interreactions of the individuals of a species in their group or societal function. You will recall that, contrary to popular assumption, Darwin did not base his principle of the survival of the fittest entirely upon the special equipment of the individual. He based it also upon this instinct of racial solidarity which, operating within the species as a whole, tends to unite and preserve the individuals composing it as a concerted biological unit or group.* This reference to the instinctive substrate of man's interreactions as it operates within social communities is made because of the pragmatic background it affords for an undertaking that rests upon a group or societal standpoint of investigation. (1928)[3]

I think we do not realize to what extent we have

---

* "Those communities," wrote Darwin, "which included the greatest number of the most sympathetic members would flourish best, and rear the greatest number of offspring." (*The Descent of Man*, 2nd edition, p. 163.)

come to employ the term group in an entirely artificial and conventional sense. The landscape gardener arranges a group of trees, the historian a group of chronological events. There may be a group of scientists or iron workers or artists. But such a grouping is entirely external and arbitrary. There is no organic inherency uniting the several elements composing such groups. What is really represented is but a collection of elements. But when we come to speak of a group represented in a colony of ants, let us say, or a herd of deer or a tribe of primitive men, we are at once connoting an assemblage of elements that is grouped into one integral whole by reason of an inner organic bond common to the several elements of which it is composed. It is this type of group that unites the elements of the species. In such organic groups the connecting link among them is an essential and instinctive one. It is not one that is separable by any arbitrary or external process of arrangement.

Naturally in a group that embodies but an arbitrary collection of individuals the part or element may be readily drawn aside and subjected to a process of isolation and examination—the process we know as analysis. Isolating the individual or part of such a conventional association of elements entails no organic breach—not any more than would the disturbance of the landscapist's arrangement of trees or the school principal's distribution of pupils. But tearing the leaves or petals from their stalk in order to analyze them is a process that necessarily severs the part under examination from functional continuity with the organic whole of which it is a part. The continuity of the organism as a whole is instantly destroyed. So with the ants removed from their colony or the deer withdrawn from their herd.

The operation of this organic group law within the life of gregarious animals is not an observation restricted by any means to the biological expert. It is a circumstance of practical utility among all intelligent keepers of wild animals. Hagenbeck is not less familiar than Darwin or Kropotkin* with the significance of this organic principle uniting the individuals of a species. But while we all tacitly admit that there is this tribal or racial instinct extending throughout and binding together the elements or individuals of a species, we have yet to recognize it within ourselves as an *organic principle of consciousness.* We have yet to see that this societal principle, observable in the spontaneous clusters of primitive man, exerts its instinctive and biological sway equally today within the life of civilized communities. (1927)[4]

Man is not an individual. His mentation is not individualistic. He is part of a societal continuum that is

---

* Footnote from *The Biology of Human Conflict,* p. 64: The first portion of Kropotkin's too little known work, *Mutual Aid* (Kropotkin, P., *Mutual Aid, A Factor of Evolution,* New York, Alfred A. Knopf, 1921) gives an excellent account of the principle of organic consistency uniting and motivating the individuals of an animal species into an integral, organismic whole. But the second half distinctly falls away in its artificial attempt to relate this biological principle of unity evidenced in animals to the quite sentimental and self-conscious expressions of "unity" that characterize civilized communities of man. In the author's effort to affiliate our widely systematized charities or the helpful community services of the social worker with the manifestations of this biological principle of mutual aid, his thesis is largely vitiated.

Heard gives evidence from various anthropological and other sources of this same organic principle as it expresses itself in primitive peoples and indicates the "complete group identity" that underlies their motivations, individual and social.

Heard, Gerald, *The Ascent of Humanity, An Essay on The Evolution of Civilization,* New York, Harcourt, Brace & Co., 1929, p. 60.

Allee, too, has offered experimental data demonstrating the principle of biological unity inherent in animal species.

Allee, W. C., *Animal Aggregations: A Study in General Sociology,* Chicago, University of Chicago Press, 1931.

the outgrowth of a primary or racial continuum. As the individual finds his basis in an individual continuum with a maternal source, so the social organism has its basis in a continuum with a phylogenetic matrix. It is my thesis that this racial continuum is the basis of man's societal life.

In recent years the attempt has been made on the part of myself and a few students to establish a means for the practical recognition among us as individual organisms of this common substrate of feeling and reaction. It has been our practical endeavor to relate individual manifestations to this common racial principle shared among us and to study the pathological divergences of our various feeling reactions in the light of this common feeling continuum. (1926)[5]

It is this group principle of coordination that represents the group basis of analysis,* as it is the images of common interchange sponsored by the social medium that represent the material to be analyzed. We should understand, however, at the outset that the social medium is represented quite as completely in the single individual as in a group of individuals, precisely as the instinctive group principle of man is embodied as fully in the single individual as in the group. In the sphere of the social medium, likewise, images that are social are necessarily personal also, just as in the sphere of man's instinctive life his phylogenetic basis is ontogenetic as well. (1928)[6]

For the individual is not just part of the species or phylum in the sense in which a domino is part of a set of dominoes. An individual organism is the outgrowth of an organismic principle of behavior that is moti-

---

* The approach introduced by Burrow-Ed.

vated within the phylum as a whole and, as an outgrowth of this phylic principle of integration, the
individual remains always an integral element within
the organism of man as a unit. The individual is himself a whole, just as the species of which he is the outgrowth is an integrated whole. As individuals we are
fundamentally not separate; we are integral wholes
within an integral whole. This is the conception we
need somehow to transmute into a physiological pattern of behavior and incorporate biologically within
ourselves as a species or phylum. (1949)[7]

A number of my correspondents have questioned
my emphasis upon the group or phylum, feeling that I
neglect the individual. But one purpose of my investigations is to find a method for freeing the individual
organism for greater creative achievements, especially
as these achievements have to do with his feeling-life,
with his artistic and cultural attainments.

The highest level of creative accomplishment is
not opposed to but consistent with the individual's
continuity with the species. In this connection, it is interesting that the words *genius* and *genus* are derived
etymologically from a common root. Our experimental
studies indicate that when man adopts a technique
that dissipates his conditioned concerns, the fullness
and continuity of his feeling-life will be restored.
These studies give full support to the position that inherently the feeling processes of individuals are continuous and consistent with one another, and that the
individual's originality, his creativeness, his rapport
with the environment is in direct proportion to his internal appreciation of this continuity. (1953)[8]

Because of the physiological consistency inhering

in the basic substance called protoplasm, there exists throughout the tissues of a species a consistent pattern of structure and function. The individual organism is a consistent unit in itself only by virtue of its consistent adherence to the pattern of structure and function that constitutes the solidarity of the species. The solidarity of individual and phylum, then, represents a biologically consistent norm of behavior. The establishment of this norm in respect to the individual was the prerequisite to the development of the medical and biological sciences. For it has been typical of these sciences that they have first determined the healthy character of the structures and functions existing within a given species, and from this universal norm have proceeded to demonstrate the nature of the processes that mark the individual's deviation from this experimentally determined constant.

As yet medicine has not recognized the need to apply this principle of an established norm to disorders occurring in the field of man's interrelational behavior. It has not recognized the principle of an established norm that holds equally for functions and reactions that interrelate the species to the environment, and for those that interrelate the organisms of the species to one another. Instead, it has permitted a purely subjective social reaction-average arbitrarily *called* "normality" to stand as the criterion of healthy human relations. (1949)[9]

Before the introduction of socially agreed signs and symbols, the organism's adjustment to its surroundings was effected, as we know, by means of certain general tensional alterations. These reactions constituted an integral or organic mode of adaptation or attention. Through this process of attention the organism as a whole encountered its environment as a whole.

In response to this integral species of attention the organism performed its various "instinctive" functions—the function of locomotion, of rest, the function of nutrition, of elimination, of herd or family interplay, of sex activity as of the corresponding interludes of sex quiescence. By virtue of these functions, alternately cumulative and dissipatory, the animal procured its food, gathered for the winter, sought shelter, found repose, grew tense or relaxed, slept or awakened. There was thus maintained that physiological balance of tensions and releases through which the total organism secured its internal adjustment to external conditions.

This organic reciprocity, this synergy between organism and environment is, of course, no less the biological basis of the organism's total function today. This organic rapport between internal tension and external stimulus tends equally today to maintain in man, as in the lower animals, a balance of adjustment between inner and outer processes. In their racial homogeneity, these internal tensions constituted for man a medium of interindividual communication as comprehensive and as efficient for the purposes of the organism as a whole as the sophisticated symbols of interchange that have come to serve as his social intercommunication today. (1932)[10]

But man has been led far from this basic norm and from an understanding of the wholeness and commonness of human motivation. In place of this whole view of whole processes, the human organism and its methods of dealing with human behavior are now everywhere divided and at odds. Yet it is useless to deal with division as it occurs in this faction or that, with the ideology of one nation as opposed to another, with the political systems that motivate the western hemisphere as contrasted with the eastern. It is as useless as the present approach to the part-reactions embodied in mental disturbances. If we are seriously to approach the problem of mental disorder, if we are really to understand, for example, the nature of the divisive part-reaction represented in schizophrenia, we shall have to begin with an understanding of the nature of man's total undifferentiated behavior as a phyloorganism. Whether it is a question of mollusc or man, science cannot understand the part until it has understood the whole. (1949)[11]

Common laws and principles are operative throughout nature. Through these laws and principles, phenomena are related effectively and meaningfully. Whether in physics, astronomy or ecology, there is a coordination of the interacting parts into a totality of structure and function. By and large, electrons and protons react in an orderly way; the stars remain within their appointed orbits; and an effective balance is maintained among the various species of organism and their environments. It is only in the field of human behavior that this primary orderliness does not seem to apply. It is only in man's relation to man that there exists confusion worse confounded. It is only here that we see impasse and over-all destructive trends. But, as C. Judson Herrick once wrote me:

> The world is not mad. It is only the people in it who are mad. The world is orderly, and even human madness is lawfully ordered. It has causes and consequences which can be discovered and ameliorated.

It is the growing view of men of science that there can

be no question as to the inherent unity of human groups throughout the world.* In *Mirror for Man,* the anthropologist Clyde Kluckhohn remarks: "The members of all human groups have about the same biological equipment."** And the renowned physiologist A.J. Carlson has said:

> We hear much today about "One World," but not enough about "One Human Species." At least we do not always act, at home or abroad, as if we believed this proved biologic fact.*** (1964)[12]

In Freud's essay, "Reflections on War and Death," there occurs a passage that points up very significantly the problem of man's interrelational discord and conflict. Says Freud, "Why it is that even in times of peace every nation and all the individuals within a nation should disdain, hate and abhor one another is indeed a mystery. I simply cannot understand it,"**** In making this statement Freud was not speaking of any insular tribe or sect. He had in mind people everywhere, the general run of individuals and groups that make up normal society. He had in mind human behavior the world over, the behavior of you and of me. In short, his thoughts were concerned with the popular social reactions of human beings whose feeling and thinking, identical with yours and mine, are those of normality.

---

* For instance, see Bohm, David: *Wholeness and the Implicate Order,* London, Boston and Henley: Routledge and Kegan Paul, 1980, p. 16.-Ed.

** New York: Whittlesey House, 1949, p. 20.

*** "Science, Education, and the Future of Man," *Scientific Monthly,* 65 (1947), p. 502

**** "Warum die Völkerindividuen einander eigentlich geringschätzen, hassen, verabscheuen, und zwar auch in Friedenszeiten, und jede Nation die andere, das ist freilich rätselhaft. Ich weiss es nicht zu sagen." Freud, Sigmund, "Zeitgemässes über Krieg und Tod," *Imago,* 1915, Vol. IV, p. 12.

Though purely academic, this question of Freud's regarding human conflict is interesting. It is a question that I too had asked myself very early in my psychoanalytic work. It happened, however, that I attempted to approach it not as a mere philosophical inquiry but as a very pressing problem in human behavior that called for precise experimental research. It was to find an answer to this question—what is the matter with normality?—that with the assistance of a few associates I undertook to investigate the basic composition of human communities or groups. We attempted to examine the phenomenon of conflict not as presented by one side or the other, but as exemplifying a state of mind that affects both sides equally. Assuming the role of voluntary guinea pigs in this research, it was our aim to discover, if possible, why there exists this social undercurrent of conflict throughout the processes of normal groups—why there exist disdain and hatred among nations and individuals throughout the world.

In order to assist our inquiry we felt the need first to determine the structure and function that enter into the formation of social units. We asked ourselves: What is the essential make-up and motivation of the behavior-aggregates composing normal communities? What is the biology of the social self and in what way may this social entity be brought to the test of scientific diagnosis and control?

Thus our group research* set out with the purpose of analyzing the current adaptation popularly classified throughout human society as "normality"—the social reaction-average which, though dubbing itself healthy, is compelled from generation to generation to

---

* This research is described in Chapter II.-Ed.

maintain permanent prisons and asylums for the individual and periodic wars for the community. (1949)[13]

Everywhere throughout "normal" society we find the counterpart of the disorders we designate clinically as hysteria, psychasthenia, schizophrenia, manic-depressive reactions, obsessive and phobic states, etc. In the larger generic view these reactions are seen to exist throughout the community. The psychiatrist who sits in his study or in the hospital clinic or at the bedside of a mentally ill patient is but one of many thousands of psychiatrists who at that moment are sitting with corresponding thousands of patients similarly afflicted. These patients represent specific social reactions to a generic social condition. It is the social condition that is the disorder. But to the individual psychiatrist the disorder of such a patient appears to be an individual disorder. From the partitive* basis of psychiatry—from the basis of the psychiatrist's social and professional habituations—the patient is unique and all-important. But the physician's partitive basis, like the patient's, is an erroneous inference based upon an erroneous social premise. It is only as we summon the broader recourses of an organismic purview that we shall recognize the narrow, unilateral premise upon which man's current social systems—political, religious, psychiatric, economic, international—now operate. (1949)[14]

Every country and every group of countries is honeycombed with economic and political ideologies that breed suspicion and disorganization throughout the life of these countries. The self-interested greed of one nation or coalition of nations is pitted against the

* In Burrow's usage, the word *partitive* refers to the limited, self-biased attitude of "normality." For a fuller definition, see Glossary.-Ed.

greed and self-interest of other nations in peace no less than in war; and among nations that are momentarily allied, it is only a matter of time before a rift that is no less arbitrary and dictatorial divides them once more. So with human relations upon every hand. It is a commonplace to see covenant turn to discord, affection and marriage ending in disaffection and divorce; international treaties dissipated in war. Labor and capital are sworn enemies, Negro and white stand in sullen opposition to one another; Jew and gentile, East and West, communism and democracy, the so-called lower and the so-called upper strata of human society are all at daggers drawn. There is conflict in the individual, in the family, in the community. Everywhere we see sectionalism and competitiveness. Everywhere the part stands against the part, and all the parts contend against the whole. No matter what the superficial pattern, there appears to be a deep-seated dislocation within the domain of human interrelations. This partitiveness, this dichotomy is not personal or local; it is universal. Apparently the very identity of individual and nation rests upon a hidden premise of division. (1949)[15]

The universality of man's increasingly disordered behavior is, in a superficial, mental sense, generally accepted. Man's contradictory behavior, his division and competitiveness, his emotional instability and general inconsistency of behavior are more or less commonly admitted. But had man a reliable scientific perspective upon these traits of his in relation to his kind, they would of themselves indicate to him a serious disturbance in organismic values. They would mean not merely a problem of the single individual, nor even a problem of man socially, but an organismic problem, a biological and physiological problem of man as a species or phylum. In short, it is not alone the superficial picture of behavior but also its basic physiological matrix that is universal. (1949)[16]

In our interindividual dilemma it is inevitable that we should find upon every hand get-together programs of amity and accord that only further augment and disguise the essential discord within the structure of man's organism as a species. Man is the only animal that goes to church, is given in marriage, is bound by sacred vows and ceremonials, contributes to worthy charities, boasts nationwide programs of mental hygiene, that has an elaborate system of traditional laws and a moral code based upon a sense of right and wrong as dictated by our "conscience."

At the same time, however, man is the only animal in whom there occur the behavior-disorders that now characterize the species throughout—hatred, competitiveness, crime, war, the neuroses and psychoses, as well as all manner of diseases, endemic and epidemic. Nowhere do we find the sharp contrasts in individual privilege, the marked differences in social well-being and security among the elements of a species that exist within the race of man. We see vast numbers of our human communities undernourished and dying for lack of sustenance or the opportunity to procure it, while side by side we see individuals possessing stores of food and comfort a hundredfold over and above the organism's needs. These ineptitudes and inequalities in man's social adjustments hardly require emphasis. The state of social chaos prevailing throughout the world today is sufficient testimony to the unhealthy condition of man's organism as a phylum. (1937)[17]

In all poetry, in all great art, as in all religions, we find allegorical expressions of the sense of man's organic unity, and we find corresponding expressions of his sense of the lack of its fulfillment. The Book of Job with its paeans of praise to the Almighty is a symbolic manifestation, albeit unconscious, of man's feeling of his own phylic integrity In Matthew Arnold's saluta- tion to the "enduring power, not ourselves, which makes for righteousness," there is but the symbolic exaltation of the power and unity of man as a phylum. The whole epic of the life and death of Christ and of the Christian ideal is again a symbolic portrayal of man's organic continuity, as also of its partitive be- trayal. One thinks, too, of the majestic epic of Aes- chylus, *Prometheus Bound;* and nothing in our own day could more beautifully symbolize the loss of the organism's primary wholeness and integrity than Francis Thompson's *Hound of Heaven.* Throughout all great literature this underlying theme of man's struggle, as of his defeat, is the substance and meaning of the folk dramatization of man's partition and neurosis. (1949)[18]

*I have thought of your comment at our last talk— that it did not seem possible that there should exist so complete a unity between any two people as the unity that exists in the common function of one's two hands. Your skepticism is most natural under the circum- stances but I think you and I have pretty definitely agreed that the "circumstances" are very far from natu- ral, owing to the habituations that have come to play so significant a part in human life as it is now understood. It is, I think, to these circumstances which are now a

---

* From a letter to William E. Galt.

part of the system about and within us that is due our skepticism.

As part of the system we favor the system. We doubt the simplicity that underlies life because we are already caught up in its complexity. Because of the system of competitiveness about us our doubt is really prompted by our prior self-interest. (1922)[19]

Several of my colleagues have called attention to fighting and other evidences of hostility in animal species, and questioned whether the disorder in behavioral adaptation emphasized by me is peculiar to man. It does seem to me that there is an evolutionary break, a definite difference between the hostility, aggressiveness and conflict which we see expressed in the interrelational behavior of man, and the fighting and aggression that are exhibited by all other animals. By and large and under natural conditions, an animal fights to procure food, to mate, or to defend itself from attack. Its fighting is a behavior-pattern that is indissolubly integrated with survival. It is closely related to the animal's total environmental reality. As evolutionary development through the ages demonstrates, it operates in a way that tends to preserve rather than to dissipate the species.

My researches clearly indicate to me that this situation has been reversed in man; that with the enhancement of individualism the balance in favor of group survival has been placed in serious jeopardy. Today the very existence of the species is threatened because the antagonisms characterizing man have been largely divorced from his biological needs and actualities. On his present basis of adaptation, man's behavior is characterized by an underlying mood of hostility, of suspicion, of competitive and destructive trends toward so-called "others," toward those outside the pale of "me" and "mine." I am reminded of a quotation from Bernard Shaw, "Man is the only animal of which I am thoroughly and cravenly afraid. I have never thought much of the courage of a lion tamer. Inside the cage he is at least safe from other men. There is less harm in a well-fed lion. It has no ideals, no sect, no party, no nation, no class; in short, no reason for destroying anything it does not want to eat." (1953)[20]

But mere concepts and commentaries, whether of scientist or layman, cannot cope with a breach in the functional integrity of man as a phyloorganism. We must look deeper than this. There is required something far more radical than mere words or concepts if medicine is to deal with the actual pathology involved in man's contradictions of behavior. We have here, as I have indicated, a problem in medicine and biology, a problem in physiology and anatomy. (1949)[21]

As government procedure is itself an expression of our divisive civilization, governmental legislation is powerless to adjust the economic and industrial disorders that are menacing the foundations of society today. Our national programs of adjustment with all their earnest intentions do not possess the scientific qualifications for providing a substantial solution of our difficulties. Nor is there anywhere extant a basis of international parley competent to relieve man's economic and social disorders upon any but a superficial and ephemeral basis.

There are unmistakable indications, however, that man's own social processes are on the threshold of a biological genesis. The signs clearly point to alterations in community-life which affect the very basis of man's interreactions. The physiological disturbance that characterizes man's functional interreactions as a race is not a circumstance for political debate or social conference. (1932)[22]

What appears to be needed in this disordered and unhappy world is a return to the organismic principle that will permit of man's conscious and intrinsic self-government. There is need, not of theoretical mechanisms or of projective preoccupations with the behavior of others, but a frank concern with the behavior of ourselves through the subjective appreciation of a disorder existing among us socially. When some years ago a few of us organized into a group of behavior-students and became the voluntary patients, individually and collectively, of the unit consisting of that same group as a societal whole, it was with a view to confronting the problem of behavior as it exists internal to man himself. Our concern was not with the deviation of the obviously disordered individual opposite us but, for all our seeming security as individuals and as a group, with a wholly unsuspected disharmony within ourselves—the social system of "normality." Regarding ourselves as integral elements within a racially organismic whole, it was our endeavor to initiate an objective inquiry into this socially continuous lamina of conflict and disbehavior. (1949)[23]

The segmented phyloorganism, like the house that is divided against itself, must fall. This is the catastrophe we are witnessing, though with unseeing eyes, in the world today. This is the real fall of man. It is no longer a matter of its mere dramatic portrayal in myth and legend, of its artistic projection in the fanciful dream of the novelist. It is a matter now of the actual fall of man, of the internal disarticulation of biosocial man as a global entity, to which we ourselves

are the unconscious witness, as we are the unconscious contributors to it. This real, this biosocial fall of
man is evidenced in the growing disintegration of
man's institutions, social, political and economic—institutions that are the sick product of our division in
feeling and motivation, of man's segmentation as a
phyloorganism. (1949)[24]

It is the nature of the organism of man that it is
one, not many; and it is likewise the nature of the sur-
rounding world that it is one, and not many. In the
complemental homeostasis between the world within
and the world without, between the internal and external environments, lies the biological health and security of man. Man's health lies not in the many false
images, not in the many Gods which in his artificial division as a species he has set up for vicarious comfort
and happiness. His health and security lies in the indivisible, organismic interaction between the unitary
principle of solidarity within the organism of man and
the harmoniously ordered universe outside him.

The organism of man is ever in its infancy and
ever achieving new maturity; but it is ever one organism, one organismic infant, one organismic adult,
one organismic species in relation to its environment.
Interrelationship is always, and first of all, between organismic man and his organismic environment. This is
primary; all else is secondary. If this primary balance
is disturbed, all else is correspondingly disturbed.
This organismic frame of reference is the requisite
basis from which man can observe and study his own
behavior. (1949)[25]

The principle of integration has throughout the
ages been the biological keystone in the development
of structural forms. This principle of integration can-

not be neglected in the developmental scheme of social man. It must be brought to bear upon the
functional life of man. It must be given dynamic
applicability to the interrelational behavior of man as a
species. (1950)[26]

   *My thesis, as I think I have told you, is not popu-
lar. But I believe it can be. I am convinced that just as
there is nothing on the instinctual level that is more
"popular," more welcome organismically than the feel
of mutuality and common kinship, so a thesis that attempts to expound the biological basis of this instinctual trend should become equally acceptable within
the community. Certainly I know of no behavioral impetus that cries out for emphasis more strongly than
this basic unity and integration inhering in the human
organism—I hope my book [*The Neurosis of Man*] can
stimulate a conscious recognition of this common
bond among us. (1945)[27]

---

* From a letter to Herbert Read.

Source Notes

[1] *The Biology of Human Conflict*, pp. 34–35

[2] *The Neurosis of Man*, pp. 3–4

[3] "The Autonomy of the 'I' from the Standpoint of Group Analysis," pp. 1–2

[4] "The Group Method of Analysis," pp. 268–70

[5] "The Laboratory Method in Psychoanalysis," p. 349

[6] "The Autonomy of the 'I'," p. 6

[7] *The Neurosis of Man*, pp. 169–70

[8] *Science and Man's Behavior*, pp. 59, 66

[9] *The Neurosis of Man*, p. 192

[10] *The Structure of Insanity*, pp. 22–24

[11] *The Neurosis of Man*, p. 318

[12] *Preconscious Foundations of Human Experience*, p. 149

[13] "The Social Neurosis," pp. 26–27

[14] *The Neurosis of Man*, p. 64

[15] *Ibid.*, pp. 24–25

[16] *Ibid.*, p. 132

[17] "The Organismic Factor in Disorders of Behavior," pp. 333–34

[18] *The Neurosis of Man*, p. 202

[19] *A Search for Man's Sanity*, p. 66

[20] *Science and Man's Behavior*, pp. 55–57

[21] *The Neurosis of Man*, p. 128

[22] *The Structure of Insanity*, p. 72

[23] *The Neurosis of Man*, p. 67

[24] *Ibid.*, pp. 301–02

[25] *Ibid.*, pp. 321–22

[26] "Prescription for Peace," p. 115

[27] *A Search for Man's Sanity*, p. 479

II

Phyloanalysis:
A Study of the Social Self

Editor's Note

This chapter describes the group analytic research instituted by Burrow and Shields; it points up
some differences between this study and later approaches such as group therapy, group encounter and
sensitivity training. A principal difference, of course,
lies in Burrow's phylic perspective itself.

This perspective requires the inclusion of the observer's own processes. Our usual method of studying
human relations, Burrow indicated in a 1925 paper,
embodies "the assumption that the position intrinsic
to the observer is an all-inclusive and authentic one.
Already it presumes a universe of which the on-
looker's own self-limited position is the basis. Whatever the point of view, it is invariably the point of
view of the observer." In the same paper, Burrow explains that his work brings a relativistic frame of reference to the study of behavior.

For Burrow, "the observer's own processes" included the physiological attitudes and sensations that
accompany observation and cognition. In fact, he
speaks of "the consciousness that is our own kinetic

function."* And he indicates in a letter to a colleague (see p. 32) that the verbal exchange at a phyloanalytic meeting is of little significance—the procedure is concerned with "the underlying feeling-content as physiologically experienced." It was with the inclusion of this "organic dimension"* that the social neurosis was to be studied.

As the word affect *appears throughout this chapter, it is clarifying for the reader to have the advantage of knowing in advance precisely what special meaning it has for Burrow—a meaning which is specific to his thought and differs from the ordinary definition of the word. For Burrow,* affect *connotes biased feeling, unwarranted emotional tone, a distortion of our native sense of oneness and affiliation. It is when such basic feeling becomes deflected to the self-image with its biased concerns and defenses that* affect *occurs.*

Burrow saw this autistic self-image—the "I"-persona—as a social phenomenon. Cherished by each individual, it is congealed within social institutions. "We came to see," he wrote, "that human society is composed of arbitrary 'I'-personae based upon an esoteric sense of right, and that we ourselves embodied just such arbitrary 'I'-personae" (p. 37).

"Each investigator finds the material of his phylobiological observations in his own reaction-patterns," he says on page 48. "But the reaction-pattern of the individual is not confined to his own behavior and, therefore, he cannot find it in himself alone. It is part of a larger social pattern. The individual and his conflict are part of a pattern that is phylic."

---

* "A Relative Concept of Consciousness," 1925, pp. 8–10.

Mental disorder is an industrial problem—a problem in how to get along. It is also an organic physiological problem—a problem in biological economy. The biological economy of an organism is the functional integrity of its parts. Mental conflict and insanity, industrial conflict and crime are disorders of economy or of adaptation that lie within us as integral parts, not outside of us as detached onlookers. They present problems not of ourselves as isolated individuals, but of ourselves as a community. They are problems in community living, in how to get along with others. These problems are physiological and economic, biological and social.

Group or social analysis* is the analysis of the immediate group in the immediate moment. A social group or community consists of persons each of whom is represented under the symbol he calls "I" or "I, myself." This proprietary symbol is socially accepted by the individuals of the group. It is the basis of their intercommunication. But the "I" that is socially accepted is socially elusive of analysis. The group composed of individual "I's" is equally elusive of social analysis. The sum of impressions symbolized as "I" would center attention everywhere else than upon the sum of impressions thus symbolized. Group analysis is the objective analysis of this subjective symbol as represented in the immediate group in the immediate moment. (1928)[1]

It may be of interest to mention briefly something of the actual situation that first led to our group basis of

---

* It was not until 1930, in "The Physiological Basis of Neurosis and Dream," that Burrow began to use the term *phyloanalysis* for his work.-Ed.

analysis (1918).* One of my patients, a student of unusual analytic insight and training, sensing the incon-
gruity in the situation, challenged the discrepancy
between my theoretical statements regarding our socially common basis of consciousness and the individualistic position which, as an analyst, I arbitrarily
continued to maintain. I was caught up by his protest
against the inconsistency of these positions and by the
interest this attitude seemed to me to offer experimentally, though unconsciously I was still skeptical of its
practical value. And so I reluctantly agreed to an arrangement whereby the student should become the
analyst and I the analysand, it being presumed that the
social basis I advocated in theory would be adopted
actually and without prejudice by him.

The arduous months of this experiment served
only to prove that the patient's opposition to the inconsistency of my personal method was actuated by an
equally personal and inconsistent method on his part
and that the theory of a social approach to individual
consciousness was no more actual in his case than in
my own.

This finding led to a further extension of our experiment which consisted in the gradual development
of a technique involving groups of individuals, first
smaller groups and finally larger, the smaller groups
consisting of as few as four, the larger of as many as
twenty individuals. In such groups there was abro-
gated entirely the distinction between analyst and
analysand, each individual automatically becoming
both. (1926)[2]

It early became clear to me that if the neurosis

---

* See Author's Preface for a more detailed description.-Ed.

were social, it was only in a social situation that one could seek a remedy for it. This view was responsible for the inception of our group analytic studies. It was imperative that the student of behavior secure conditions that would afford him social cooperation in his effort to make objective his habitually subjective trends. I felt that he should have conditions that would not only leave him free to voice whatever evidence of partitive feeling in himself or others the laboratory setting offered him, but that by the very terms of the laboratory technique he should feel himself under scientific obligation to do so. (1949)[3]

Our preliminary purpose was to lay bare as far as possible the primary elements entering into the behavior of ourselves, as individuals and as groups, quite in defiance of habitual *mores* or the traditional prejudices with which we found ourselves shackled, but which we now recognized as the common heritage of us all. In this social process our effort was directed towards divorcing ourselves from the medium of habituations that now constitutes the basis of man's personal orientation and security—from our socialized opinions, judgments, moralisms, dependencies and beliefs. (1949)[4]

Our group process was not concerned with differentiations between socially approved and socially disapproved behavior, between "right" and "wrong," between neurotic and normal, man and woman, white and negro, or between people who are "important" and people who are not "important." Nor was it concerned with any other of the blighting dichotomies with which man is socially beset upon every side. The common denominator recognized by our research unit was not the individual or a collection of individuals, but organismic man—the phylum of man as a whole. (1949)[5]

In seeking material requisite to our investigation of human behavior and its disorders, it was not necessary to go beyond the confines of our own research group. As a social group we ourselves constituted the experimental material for studying the behavior-reactions of man at large. While our own group-behavior was not more disordered than the behavior of any other social group, it was imperative that in attempting to deal phylobiologically with subjective anomalies of behavior, the subjects embodying these phenomena apply their examination to themselves—to their own subjective reactions. For the circumstance is inescapable that only a subject's own experiential self presents immediate behavior-material. It is this immediate material that has occupied the biosocial investigations of my associates and myself as constituting the only material that satisfies the conditions of an exact scientific inquiry into man's behavior. (1949)[6]

Biologically, any human group is a cross section of human society, and human society is but another name for the species man. Our experimental set-up, then, consisted of a minute section of the species man; and the aspect of the section under investigation was the functional interaction or the social behavior of the section as a whole and of the separate individuals composing the section. We ourselves—the physicians, students and patients participating in the investigation—were the material under investigation. We were both agent and receptor. We were the investigators, but we were also the material to be investigated. Our task was to observe as a whole organism, individual and social, whatever partitive function was perceptible within the individual or within the unit as a whole. (1950)[7]

*Our whole position rests upon the inversion of the customary analytic relationship in which the analyst stands as critique toward the individual analysand. On the contrary, in our laboratory outlook the united societal consciousness composing our group becomes the critique in respect to the individual, be this individual the medical colleague represented in Freud, or yourself, or myself or anyone else; and, correspondingly, in the interest of his laboratory investigation, the medical colleague submits himself *as a patient* to be investigated by this societal consciousness. I wish it might be possible for me to make clear to you that the analysis of a group *by me,* the individual, or the analysis of a group even by Professor Freud, the individual, cannot possibly interest us as laboratory investigators. In our group approach what can alone be of interest to me as a laboratory investigator is the group's analysis of me. What can alone be of interest to Professor Freud or to you as laboratory investigators is the group's analysis of him or of you. From a laboratory point of view I cannot be interested in Professor Freud's interpretations or in my own when we stand before the group as teachers or physicians. What interests me is the group's interpretation of Professor Freud or of me, when we stand before the group as quite isolated and "normal" individuals requiring for our essential integrity of personality the coherence of man's original group or societal basis. (1926)[8]

Our colleagues continue to assume that we do not differ from the group-therapists who try to bring their

---

* From a letter to Paul Federn, M.D. (a colleague of Sigmund Freud).

patients to react in a more "mature" and more "normal" manner. With my associates and myself, however, the essential point is precisely that the presumably "mature and normal manner" is the whole trouble; and as for "guidance," any such interference with other people's thinking or feeling or doing is, in the very premise of phyloanalysis, automatically excluded. (1949)[9]

*The data obtained in group analysis—the data being the feeling-reactions of the organism as expressed physiologically in the immediate moment—do not of their nature lend themselves to reportorial account. The immediate physiological moment, when reported in intellectual or verbal symbols, ceases of course to be the immediate physiological moment. I can tell you *about* the reaction or event *after* its occurrence but I cannot possibly impart to you the event itself, and it is the event itself that you and I and our colleagues are interested in getting the actual sense of in the actual situation.

You see, the reactions that occur in group analysis are quite aside of—quite apart from the mental or intellectual sphere of our habitual social reactions. In the social or group setting, verbal material expresses the purely manifest content of the social group and it is only with the latent reactions—the emotional or feeling substrate—that group analysis is concerned. While a dictograph would record the words of the group meeting, it happens that the words, or the mental content expressed in a group meeting, are the discarded by-products of the procedure, while the underlying

---

* From a letter to Dr. Thomas D. Eliot, who had suggested that Dr. Burrow present a transcript or recording of a group analytic session at a meeting of the American Sociological Society.-Ed.

feeling-content as physiologically experienced is the only usable material. A dictographic record, therefore, would give to the meeting you propose the *words* or the merely *manifest material*; a dictograph would not reproduce the subjective physiological tensions and alterations which are the material of our group investigations. (1930)[10]

Unlike prevailing methods of procedure in psychotherapy, including my own traditional trend, phylobiology did not set out knowing in advance what was the desired goal for either the individual or the group. We sought merely to clear away whatever elements obstructed man's path to the recognition of what that goal might prove to be. There was no "normal," no gratuitously assumed social reaction-average to pin our faith to or direct our efforts towards. Our ultimate finding, like that of the early bacteriologists, was admittedly an unknown quantity. Like theirs, ours was a field of original research. And so, adhering strictly to our experimental basis, we sought to maintain an open mind as to what we might find to be the natural interrelational function of man— his basic feeling and motivation—when the artificialities that now submerge this function should be eliminated. (1949)[11]

In the course of our analysis we came to recognize the parallel that exists between the reaction of the experimentally conditioned animal in its laboratory compartment and the reactions occurring in the natural confines in which the activities of man have become spontaneously conditioned—the home, the school, the office, the industrial plant, our halls of Congress and the United Nations Security Council. In accordance with the conditions of this experimental set-up, our procedure entailed the consistent frustration of both alternatives of the conditioned reaction: Through session after session of laboratory analysis it involved the frustration of the socially ambivalent affects* and prejudices (differentially conditioned reflexes) that occur habitually in groups or communities. So that the "good" response and the "bad" were equally objects of challenge. It was not only the subjectively "wrong" affect or the socially incriminating response that constituted the object of our experimental interest, but the subjectively "right" or socially approved behavior-reaction received equal consideration in our objective inquiry. (1949)[12]

Our experimental groups, then, came together for the purpose of observing our division, our internal lack of social balance and accord. Each of us was automatically thrown back upon himself to find his way through the maze of his own unwarranted affect-projections, of his own spurious thinking and feeling. Certainly, such a process did not make for the "unity," for the "love and confidence" within our groups that one ordinarily understands by these terms. On the contrary, our procedure was a direct challenge to all that we knew as unity, to all that we knew as trust or human affection. There was no leaning upon others, or rather the habit of leaning upon others as commonly expressed throughout normality was at all times material for observation in a social system shot through with pathological moods of transference and dependence. Each of us had to make his own research in his own way at his own desk—his desk being his own organism. (1949)[13]

---

* Burrow's special use of the word *affect* is presented in the Glossary as well as in the Editor's Note, p. 26.-Ed.

As an experimental group, it was necessary to nurture our condition if we were to study it. And so, we had to remain together, to stick close day in and day out—at meals, in the instrumental laboratory, in the office and in my study. In other words, we had to invite and foster an experimental dilemma. (1953)[14]

Very early in our group investigations of systematized affect or prejudice, we were brought face to face with the dualistic nature of the prevailing precept governing the behavior of human communities—the precept subjectively experienced by everyone as a sense of right and wrong. As we know, all man's civil laws have their origin in this moral precept—the laws governing the conduct of individuals in the ownership of property, in their marriage relation and in their responsibility toward children. Among the vast majority of people in the world, this "right" is not infrequently vested in anthropomorphic gods upon whose will depends their eternal salvation or pain. Upon this sense of right rests the relation of individuals and of nations to one another. Subservience to this moral precept is the very conscience of man. But this commonly accepted sense of right governing human relations, we found, possesses a defect so fundamental as to impair its validity. It seemed to us, therefore, that in this false sense of right and wrong there might lie a clue to the common denominator in human pathology for which we were looking.

As I hope to show, the principle that underlies the prevailing dichotomy of right and wrong is fundamentally sound; it is man's misapplication of this principle that is defective and false. As now applied, this sense of right and wrong may be differently interpreted by different persons and by the same person under different circumstances. So that, far from providing a stable criterion for the adjustment of human behavior, this social determinant of values is mutable and arbitrary. In respect to evaluations of individual conduct, everyone feels that *his* opinion is correct. At any time and under any circumstances I may claim that *I* am right in my judgment regarding the conduct of other people or myself. And where this assumption of mine is participated in by others, they are regarded by *me*, by every "me," as also right. Contrariwise, those who fail to agree with me are not right. They are wrong. Thus, in my wishful mood, I arbitrarily project favor or blame, rightness or wrongness upon other people; and other people, of course, exercise this same interrelational mood prerogative in respect to me.

This circumstance prevails for any "I" or any "me," for any community or any nation. I am speaking, of course, of a generic *I*, of a generic *me*. I am speaking of the secondary, wishful entity defined in phylo-pathology as the "I"-persona.* The "I"-persona with its artificial system of interrelationships has built up in man a false, partitive sense of identity, and this false sense of identity is social in its scope. Surely, we need no more dramatic example of this arbitrary "I"-persona with its subjective dichotomy of right and wrong than is to be seen today in the obstinate mood impasse between Russia and her satellites on the one hand, and the Western allies on the other—between one half the world and the other half. (1950)[15]

Says this social substantive: *I* belong to the only true church; *I* always pay my bills promptly; *I* like to

---

* The Latin, *persona* (English, *person*) means a mask or "false face." Thus "persona," regarded as a separate motivational unit, implies semblance rather than reality. (See Glossary.-Ed.)

be entirely independent; *I* never repress my children. And so on *ad infinitum.* Of course, the "I" changes form when someone other than oneself becomes the social substantive. It then becomes you, he or she, or some proper name may stand for it. But while this "I," "you," "he," "she," "John," or "James" is the symbol under which we designate one another (just as we designate the countless objects about us), we must not forget that each "you," "he" or "she" is the same "I" when speaking in his own right. It is merely the form that is changed when one social substantive stands, as he supposes, opposite another. (1930)[16]

Applying ourselves to the analysis of our own group—family and students, associates and myself— as constituting a cross section of human society, we came to see that the vast interrelationships of man are composed of affective *me's* and *you's* and their separative mood projections. We came to see that human society is composed of arbitrary "I"-personae with their artificial agreements and disagreements based upon an esoteric sense of right, and that we ourselves embodied just such arbitrary "I"-personae. This false premise of behavior stems from an impaired generic mood that is inconsistent with a basic principle of solidarity and cooperation among individuals and communities. For, where other people do not agree with *my* arbitrary and sovereign sense of what is right, there is enmity. Where other communities or nations fail to agree with this arbitrary sense of right on the part of *my* community or nation, there is war. (1950)[17]

Lacking the motivation or behavior that is physiologically continuous, having substituted the premise that the organism's motivation rests upon a basis that is private and dichotomous, our reactions can only be private and dichotomous also. We may only *deal with* one another; we may not be *united as* one another. If there is conviviality and accord, it is not because of a phylic union between the organisms involved, but because momentarily the self-interest of each of us happens to correspond in its outward form. Beneath this outer suavity there is inner conflict, and this hidden conflict entails a constant attitude of diplomacy. It entails a studied concealment of the ulterior aim lying beneath a relationship that rests upon two secretly opposed directions of self-interest. (1949)[18]

I have spoken many times of man's automatic defense-reactions in support of the accustomed habits and mores characteristic of the "normal" level of adaptation. It seemed to us profitable to try to discover what lay beneath this protective social covering. And so, in spite of the relentless opposition among us, in spite of our own confirmed "normality" and its inexorable "rightness," we continued to probe day after day into the underlying processes of our so-called normal behavior.

After the travail of much painstaking research it became apparent, as I have indicated, that beneath this artificial criterion of behavior and its autocratic inconsistencies there was to be found a monstrous social mood—an unrecognized mood of systematized prejudice and absolutism.

For a long time the "I"-complex or "I"-persona and its autocratic mood proved itself a match for all our efforts to reach and understand it. Nothing entered into or touched this deep-seated mood with its implicit "I"-versus-"you" dichotomy. It was as if the specious form of community conditioning embodied in the "I"-persona or in the state of mind of "normality" were the expression of a vast and compactly interknit social dissociation.* (1949)[19]

The systematized "I"-persona, the authoritarianism that arrogates to itself rights which are absolute and unimpeachable in respect to others, is the meaning of prejudice. This false sense of the self explains why prejudice and not reason is the universal authority over man's processes today. Because of prejudice, because of affect projection** and the moral dichotomy of "right" and "wrong," man's social behavior has become political instead of organismic, ulterior rather than unitary. (1950)[20]

In confronting this spurious criterion now everywhere activating human behavior, it was our effort to discover and credit whatever healthy behavioral elements remained as a residue after we had eliminated these specious standards. In other words, our objective procedure led us to seek a basis of discrimination between disorganized or deviate behavior and organized or healthy behavior—a basis that would disavow the commonly alleged difference between one individual and another, between one group or nation and another, upon grounds of the specially claimed prerogative of each. Repudiating habitual moralisms, the method of phyloanalysis made evident a condition of organization or unity of function that extends throughout the species or phylum as a whole, while parallel with this unitary principle of behavior there

---

* The development of this social dissociation is discussed in Chapter III. -Ed.

** According to Hinsie and Campbell's *Psychiatric Dictionary, Third Edition* (New York: Oxford University Press, 1960), *projection* refers to the process of throwing out upon another the ideas or impulses that belong to oneself, presumably those one considers undesirable.-Ed.

was likewise traceable throughout the species a system of reactions that is deviate and disorganized. (1949)[21]

In the conditioned dog there is a situation that, in the main, sufficiently resembles the situation in conditioned man to invite comparison. There is much to consider before we can claim this similarity, but for the moment, let us take an instance in the behavior of man that is analogous to that of the conditioned dog. A man builds a house. The house is good; it shelters and protects him. Along comes a friend who, as it happens, is a competent architect, and says, "I don't like the house." Says the owner, "This is my house. If you don't like it, go your way." There is defense and offense on the part of both, and in a moment both are angry. The house is still a good house that shelters and protects, but suddenly a difference has arisen subjectively between the two men that has nothing to do with the original actuality of the object, house. A "right" opinion (an affect or prejudice) has interposed. The building is no longer a mere house. To the angry owner it is *my* house—my possession. To the angry friend or architect it is also now not a house. For him, too, it is a possession; it is *his* reputation or authority as an architect. It is now the house equally of two identical "I"-personae whose unilateral interests or "rights" stand to one another in the relation of a mutually obdurate dichotomy. In the eyes of the owner, *the* house has been replaced by *my* house. In the eyes of the architect, *the* house has been replaced by *my* opinion. With both, a conditioning stimulus has been substituted for an object of reality, much as in the case of the dog a bell has been substituted for a delectable bit of meat. (1949)[22]

Phyloanalysis shows that this sense of one's "right" or prestige* is the most cherished of all human prejudices. The measures we adopt for its protection and security now operate automatically among us. These measures are both defensive and offensive. The defensive mechanism is seen in one's effort to achieve credits, to be thought approvingly of, to be "somebody." The offensive aspect of the mechanism is shown in the tendency to disparage others, to indulge in personal criticism and irritation towards them.

Affect or prejudice is a heavier blight upon the processes of man than he at all suspects. We do not think with our minds but with our prejudices. You do this, I do it, everyone does it. Two people may look at the same thing and see something quite different because of the difference in the prejudices with which they "think." Because of prejudice our mental concepts are falsely colored, our minds biased, our feelings divided, our thought refracted, our facts fractional.** (1949)[23]

It may be profitable to consider the behavior phenomenon of war in relation to the basic balance of the organism expressed in the function of homeostasis. Wars are fought between opposed factions or nations, each of which is assured that its own side is "right," while the opposed side is attempting to violate its right and is therefore "wrong." This attitude of private right is, of course, equally obdurate in the opinion of each contending party. In this way we have two socially opposed blocs, masses or systems of "rightness."

---

* Prestige (distinction or reputation) < L. *praestigium*, a delusion.

** The words *fact* and *faction* have a common origin in the Latin *facere*.

If we will look into the essential element underlying this divisive phenomenon of national or social rightness, we shall find that it arises from an early bias on the part of each individual with respect to his own prior and private privilege.* This early induced systematization is the substance of the authoritarian persona which in the tenuous scheme of human relations is commonly ensconced within each individual, group or nation.

This subjectively systematized persona is the stuff of which the dictators are fashioned, but it is equally the stuff of the dictatees. On the basis of man's social reaction-average each of us combines within his own processes the ambivalent elements of dictator and dictatee. In the behavior of each individual there is embodied this same irreconcilable discrepancy in motivation and outlook. Phyloanalysis has made evident that this complemental relation between dictator and dictatee expressed in community clusters is traceable to the systemization we embody socially as "right and wrong." (1941)[24]

To discuss the theory of the conflct involved in *my* right versus *your* right, however, is very different from participating in the actual experimental setup adopted by my associates and myself. It is one thing to talk about the obdurate mood implicit in the esoteric sense of right and wrong, but to be actually brought up against the emotional content of this dualistic premise in the heat of one's own implication in it is quite another. In our experimental work we were compelled to come to grips with this mood in all its despotic au-

---

* "Private" is from Latin, *privus*, meaning set apart, separated. "Privilege" is from Latin, *privus* (private plus *lex*, law), hence a private law, or prerogative.

thoritarianism. Theoretically, we could readily appreciate the biological falsity of our right-wrong sense of personal and social values, but we still continued to maintain our arbitrary mood habituations. When it came to the question of human behavior and to legislating as to the rights of others in relation to one's own, we were no more representative than the groups composing our national congresses or other political gatherings. In our lack of a stable, scientific criterion, our behavior was as unilateral in its motivation as that which has characterized the delegates to the United Nations parleys with their right-wrong premise of adjudication. Nevertheless, to lock oneself in a house for years with associates and students, with normal and neurotic personalities, all of whom have voluntarily pledged themselves to a schedule of unremitting challenge of their own habitual reactions, personal and social, is an experimental discipline that definitely gives pause to one's customary prepossessions—to one's reflex affects and projections. (1950)[25]

*Let us for the moment leave "pathology" as you and I have ordinarily understood it; let us return to your letter and my letter, disregarding the content of either in the ordinary sense. Let us rather take for granted quite tentatively for the moment that ideas dealing with ideas, emotions dealing with emotions *are* our human pathology. This will help us come nearer to a mutual understanding of what I would like to say. It may pave the way to something more concrete.

If there was a note of resentment in a letter I thought I had written you with feelings of only the

---

* From a letter to Dr. Adolf Meyer.

deepest cordiality and appreciation; if Dr. Syz* took an
attitude of emotional criticism toward some remarks
once made by you; if Mr. Shields* was so involved in
affect as once to have dismissed as insignificant an attitude presented by you; if the excited young woman
at the lunch table here a week ago shouts out against
me, accusing me of using the utmost craftiness and
diplomacy in my efforts to maintain the integrity of
this or that social unit or group (and incidentally never
was truer word spoken!)—none of this on the principle
now employed is of meaning. It possesses no dependable basis of experimentation and inquiry. My affect or
resentment is the symptom of a condition or disparity
circumscribed within my own organism. Likewise for
Dr. Syz, likewise for Mr. Shields, and likewise for the
student who featured in last Sunday's episode. The
condition cannot be socially projected and cannot
therefore be met with social measures of interchange
and projection—with ideas and meanings.

Since I first took up this work, now many years
ago, the affect that has piled up within and about me
has been immeasurably intense and insistent. The
problem has been forced into the acutest possible
issue and sustained at this point day in and day out
(night in and night out, too) over the years. But it is extraordinary what modifications and adjustments of
feeling and expression have occurred within the organism—the organism which, by virtue of the rigid
premise of experimentation it has more and more
made its own, *shall not speak,* shall not throw the bur-
den of complaint or question upon other speaking,
complaining, questioning persons with their habitual

---

* Associates in the phyloanalytic investigation.-Ed.

basis of interchange and understanding in the projected idea or emotion.

This will be of interest to you: In our effort to get down to an organic basis, to efface entirely the emotional basis that can project itself socially in ideas and words, none of the nice things we do and think were, in our experimental groups, admitted as any evidence of the actual sanity or integrity of the organism. Correspondingly all of the unseemly, cruel, self-satisfying, narcissistic things we fantasy "but would not do for the world" were placed in the category of things actually done. There was no alibi. Fantasy as something detached, cut off from actual motor disfunction was for practical experimentation completely unadmitted. But the intolerable shocks of this working premise were slowly preparing the organism for new and unexpected powers of adjustment.

For Mr. Shields or for Dr. Syz or for me to reabsorb this affect of ours (habitually projected by the individual into the idea or social image where it has for thousands of generations sought vent, appeasement or requital in response to a race-old habit), this is the conscious technique upon which we are at work as a directive social process.

The student who is a newcomer, relatively speaking, to our bivouac and who cries out upon my social premeditations and adroitness, finds no opposition to her opposition, no defense or extenuation, no "comeback"; her whole emotional content is utterly nugatory. Not what I do or ought to do, as *seen* by her, is her task. But to realize that her invariable preference, her automatic, reflex preference, is outward toward the projected social image, this is her task, as it is mine, Dr. Syz', Mr. Shields'. It is to integrate her own processes so that no "idea of reference"—no *emotion of reference* really—shall, as it were, slip from under the protectorate of the organism as a whole.

As words all of this is utterly meaningless. As an idea going from a me to a you it takes along no cargo whatsoever. But in the measure in which the underlying principle is your own organically, in the measure in which it is mine organically, it makes for a really powerful social force freighted with no limit of possibility, it seems to me, for social unity and integration on every hand. (1931)[26]

It may be said that in its subjective implications our experimental frustration of the affect may be compared with the objective induction of pain which the physiologist, Henry Head, experimentally imposed upon himself.* While our group purpose was not primarily, or indeed secondarily, the induction of distress or pain, it was definitely our purpose to intercept whatever deflections of feeling—no matter how pleasant or habitual—evidenced themselves in personal and social affect. This process necessarily entailed marked mental and emotional discomfort. Such a reaction, however, was but an experimental by-product of our group procedure. (1949)[27]

It is inconsequential that in our experimental groups the student at first consistently made a fiasco of the opportunity to break through the social covenants commonly posited by accepted social custom. It is inconsequential that at times he was driven to affront egregiously the amenities of orderly social interchange. For it was inevitable that at the outset he should fail to present his criticisms objectively, that he

* Head, Henry, *Studies in Neurology*, London, Oxford University Press, 1920, Vol. I, pp. 225–329.

should invariably have been prompted by motives other than those of calm, objective observation. Often enough as a matter of fact, he was "mad enough to bite," and in his extremity would, time and again, vent his wrath in tones characteristic of irritation and self-righteous resentment. It could not have been otherwise.

But it was only through such social awkwardness that the student was ultimately led to his phylobiological quarry, to his cultivation of an objective attitude toward habitually subjective reactions—reactions which in every instance we found to be based upon the absolute authority of an autocratic and imperialistic "I"-persona resident within oneself. (1949)[28]

In our group experiments, the subject whose false identity or "I"-persona was under challenge invariably reacted, as I have indicated, with intense and blind irritation against the challenger. His self-defense was immediate and automatic. But after much travail and unproductive effort, the poignancy of which can hardly be conveyed in this brief communication, we realized that this condition, internal to the self and inaccessible to every other self, could be reached only within the subject's internal processes *as a group organism.* Such a basic, generic challenge began gradually to bring each of us back to the internal cause of his own irritation and defense, to the absolutism and insubordination of his own "I"-persona. As I said, it is very easy for one person to "observe" affect irritation in another person. But the situation is quite different in which a student acknowledges irritation in himself on the evidence of the inclusive, generic mood of a research group which regards the student's irritation objectively through recognizing this same irritation within itself as a group organism. This is the situation embodied in phyloanalysis. So that my work with groups—with the reaction of man as a total organism—persistently enlisted my interest in a socially encapsulated mood that I shared equally with my associates. (1950)[29]

It is a far cry from the psychiatrist's theoretical concept of the "ego" to the internal awareness of the self—the self of *me*, or the "I"-persona. This distinction is one which we psychiatrists, like everybody else, need somehow to learn. We shall learn it, however, not from the written page but only through consistent work *internal to ourselves*. One's real knowledge of behavior must be achieved through observation of one's own processes. Today psychiatrists not infrequently voice such expressions as "we are all more or less neurotic," or "we don't know the first thing about mind and how it works." Quite true. But those who make these statements have not compassed the real truth of them. They have not come by them through a scientific reckoning with the inhibitions that obstruct our "knowing the first thing" about the workings of the human mind on the basis of our present psychiatric knowledge. Such comments lack internal substance. They are not spawned of a student's serious analysis of the multitudinous conflicts within the precious citadel of the self as they may be brought to objective awareness in the laboratory of human behavior. (1949)[30]

Our investigations demand in a very special sense the initiative of each investigator. Each investigator finds the material of his phylobiological observations in his own reaction-patterns. But the reaction-pattern of the individual is not confined to his own behavior and, therefore, he cannot find it in himself alone. It is part of a larger social pattern. The individual and his conflict are part of a pattern that is phylic. Man's behavioral *faux pas* cannot be limited to any specific element, to any special personality, community or nation. It is a *faux pas* of the species as a whole. As part of the whole, the individual is inevitably part of the disorder affecting the whole and he necessarily shares equally with others the responsibility of its investigation. In this way our research becomes the spontaneous investigation, by individual and group, of an internal conflict embodied in our common phylic reactions. (1949)[31]

Thus, our investigations of group reactions forced the problem of human relations back to a problem internal to us as a group. It became recentered within the organism from which the affect mood had been projected. And coincident with this development, there occurred an interesting phenomenon. Blocking our habitual affect projections and confining our intransigent mood within our own organisms automatically transmuted the sensation of affect into a direct sensation of stress or tension situated within the anterior cephalic zone. Instead of a falsely projected internal mood, there was now in its place the perception of the somatic reaction concomitant to it. What had been an *inter*relational conflict became an *intra*relational conflict. (1950)[32]

*I've found assistance this way in the last days. Come close now and listen. Give your mind—the mind of your organism—a chance. Over there, let us say, I see an angry man. What I "see" of course are certain external appearances—sharp, intense, narrowed

---

* From a letter to his daughter.

eyes, congested face, heightened breathing, clenched fists, etc., etc. These gestures are what I *see*. From this I *infer* the anger—from this I know the man is angry— that he has the feeling of anger within him. Very well then I do not see—do not observe the actual state of anger. Now as a scientist, dealing with man's feeling interchange as a social organism, it is necessary to observe actual material. That is how the biological scientist proceeds in the sphere of his external objective data—that is the method of the chemist and the astronomer, and so it must be the method of the group- or phylo-analyst. He must also observe direct material.

All observation hitherto has been dependent upon the external senses—anger, the feeling, isn't observable through the external senses—through the ordinary channels of perception. We've just seen that I only "infer" the feeling of which I see the external signs. How do I infer it? Through the relation between such external signs and the sensation of anger as I have experienced it within myself, or subjectively. Very well, then it is within myself that I would best observe the sensation of anger. But observation as I have known it has been a projective act hitherto. My external sense— my eye—has observed only what is before it. Like the camera that doesn't take a picture of the photographer behind it, my eye does not see or photograph feelings or conditions lying back of it. Very well then, to see or observe my anger (it might as well be love, or suspicion or greed of course) my position of observation must move back to some point or zone where it will have the anger-feeling in front of it. And so, resting back, as it were, upon the organism's primary sensation as a whole—upon the zone of primary body-feeling—one senses, at first very vaguely and fleetingly, certain sensations *in front of it*, that is, in the region of the head or cerebral zone—particularly in the region within and around the eyes. And he comes upon this extraordinary observation—that all the emotions which he believed to be biological and organic do not occupy his organism as a whole, but are centered around the eyes (chiefly) and are perceptible as certain definite tensions and constraints within that zone! No matter what the emotion—whether pleasurable or distressing—it is now objectively perceived as a sensation of stress about or within the eyes.

Now coincidentally with this shifting of the perceptual feeling-zone into the primary body-zone, there is a quiet, inclusive, self-possessed feeling or reaction. One gets a sense of having really never "seen" (as he thought) anger or love or desire, he gets a sense of the utter artificiality of his relationship to others (and to himself) on the basis of this sort of "seeing" or "feeling." He has been living—experiencing feeling—in front of his eyes, outside of himself, of his organism, where no living or feeling exists. It is really so simple but not without procuring another camera and setting it back where one may get a picture of the photographer—Mr. Man—who has hitherto been taking pictures of everyone else! You and I and the rest of us being Mr. Man. (1931)[33]

Source Notes

1   "The Basis of Group Analysis," p. 198
2   "The Laboratory Method in Psychoanalysis," p. 353
3   *The Neurosis of Man*, p. 326
4   *Ibid.*, pp. 110–11
5   *Ibid.*, p. 89
6   *Ibid.*, p. 18
7   "Prescription for Peace," p. 107
8   *A Search for Man's Sanity*, pp. 126–27
9   *The Neurosis of Man*, p. 91
10 *A Search for Man's Sanity*, pp. 233–34
11 *The Neurosis of Man*, p. 113
12 *Ibid.*, pp. 150–51
13 *Ibid.*, p. 327
14 *Science and Man's Behavior*, p. 96
15 "Emotion and the Social Crisis," pp. 467–69
16 "Physiological Behavior-Reactions in the Individual
      and the Community," p. 73
17 "Emotion and the Social Crisis," pp. 469–70
18 *The Neurosis of Man*, p. 111
19 "The Social Neurosis," pp. 28–29
20 "Prescription for Peace," p. 103
21 *The Neurosis of Man*, p. 17
22 *Ibid.*, p. 141
23 *Ibid.*, p. 39
24 "Neurosis and War," pp. 238–39
25 "Emotion and the Social Crisis," pp. 476–77
26 *A Search for Man's Sanity*, pp. 241–43
27 *The Neurosis of Man*, pp. 111–12
28 *Ibid.*, pp. 326–27
29 "Emotion and the Social Crisis," pp. 477–78
30 "The Social Neurosis," p. 31
31 *The Neurosis of Man*, p. 22
32 "Emotion and the Social Crisis," pp. 478–79
33 *A Search for Man's Sanity*, pp. 237–38

III

Origins of a Social Neurosis

Editor's Note

This chapter offers a theoretical basis for the inception of such expressions of social pathology as delinquency, crime, war and insanity. Burrow relates the beginning of such aberration in our species to an accidental development concomitant with the use of symbol and language.* For as symbolic processes developed, with their selective, discriminatory function, a gradual split occurred in our original solidarity of mood. Feeling became inappropriately attached to the symbol and no longer served as a sound motivating force.

This internal defect is inculcated anew in each generation. Burrow here describes how the parental generation inadvertently distorts the child's native interest, even while transmitting practical information needed by the child for survival.

Burrow's confidence that this condition of dis-

---

* Some contemporaries of Burrow—for instance, Ludwig von Bertalanffy and Alfred Korzybski—as well as later writers have also stressed the relationship of language to social problems. (See von Bertalanffy, L., "A Biologist Looks at Human Nature." *Scientific Monthly* 82:33–41 (1956); and Korzybski, A. *Science and Sanity*, The International Non-Aristotelian Library Publishing Company, 1933, pp. 798.)

ease, widespread though it is, may still be brought under control, is reiterated in this chapter. "There is within man's physiological organism as a race a basic health or fitness that cannot be wholly extinguished," he writes on p. 69.

The thesis of phylobiology, or the thesis of man's social development as a species, begins with the beginning of language. The philologists tell us that language probably arose some two million years ago.

It might seem, then, that we are attacking a problem that is largely archaic, theoretical, remote. It would indeed seem so but for one noteworthy circumstance—that in each generation language arises anew in each individual. It is taught afresh to every child by every parent. Our investigation, therefore, has to do with a behavior process which, far from being historic or archaic, is in fact the immediate experience of us all. Like other variations within a species, language is both immediate and remote. It denotes a process that is ontogenetic as well as phylogenetic, individual as well as social.

It is a ready habit with us to "think" of language as a discrete, individual process, rather than as the function of the species as a continuous and solidaric organism. This discrepancy is not difficult to explain. After all, it is as talking animals that we grew up, and in our daily use of language it is natural that we should take the function of speech for granted. And so we do not experience the spoken word as our interrelational selves in action. We do not sense its physiological depth and scope as a behavioral reaction within a total behavioral frame or pattern, under whose immanent sovereignty the word or symbol subsists, and to whose function as a whole it is constantly beholden.

In our study of language as a phyloorganismic process, and in our study of the influence of this process upon human behavior, let us begin, then, at the beginning. Let us begin where the race of man begins, and where we and our children begin from generation to generation in the use of this symbolic part-function. (1950)[1]

Each of us from his earliest years is educated in the use of the names or symbols of things. Each object that we see is given its corresponding sound, and we in turn reproduce this sound in designating the object to others. When we consider it, life among civilized societies is lived almost wholly in a medium of symbols. The anthropological importance of the symbol as a time- and labor-saving device need hardly be pointed out. It affords man a shorthand means of communication that is an incalculable asset to the individual and the species. However, we shall consider indications that the undue interpolation of the processes of mentation characterizing man's projective linguistic function caused a breach in the organism's physiological basis of continuity that seriously impaired its original behavior consistency. (1964)[2]

In the early life of the race, the impressions that came from the environment were common to all individuals. They were generic impressions or impressions affecting the species throughout. Among these common impressions were sunshine and darkness; the color and stir of day; the stillness of night; skies, clear or clouded; the sun's rising and setting; starlight; the smell of earth; the flow of rivers; the wide expanse of oceans, forests, plains, lakes and mountains. There were rain and wind, snow and mist, days of calm and of tempest. These phenomena of nature were a part of man's forebears. They did not *think* of them. There had not yet evolved the instrument of thinking that made possible the use of symbol or language. There was not yet full development of the special mechanism within the head of each individual that gave names to

these outer manifestations common to generic experience. The organism was not yet related to its surroundings in any projective, abstract sense. In the
beginning, it was only as a unitary whole that primitive man looked out on and reacted to his environment.

Thus, man and his environment were closely interknit, and all impressions were shared by all members of the species. Sensations were also shared—the
sensation of warmth and cold; of strength, fleetness
and agility; the reactions to food, sounds, odors, activity and rest. In his phyletic infancy, as in his larval
state individually, man dwelt in a natural continuum
with the conditions about him. That is, the whole experience of his common perception of the objects
about him was a sensation, a physiological aspect, of
himself. Man's relation to his kind and to his environment constituted for him an undifferentiated *intra*relationship.

In this early season of man's growth, processes of
thought had not yet differentiated or set apart any individual or group of individuals. Just as sensations and
impressions were experienced by all men, so were
man's interests and motivations—the interest of play
and work, of security against the severity of winter; the
provision of shelter and warmth; the physiological releases induced periodically by the instinctual drives of
mating and reproduction on which the continuity of
generations depends. These actions were all genuine
physiological responses of an organic nature, arising
from man's needs.

With the common awareness of these phenomena,
there was also the sense of man's own commonness.
The impressions and sensations and the interests they
awakened commonly in man ever served the integra-

tion and consolidation of man as a whole, as a unitary organism. The compactness of man and environment was continuous with the relationship of the individual and his kind.

In this powerful bond, this continuity between objective sensations and subjective feelings, between the earth and man's own physiological processes, we may come upon the primary pattern of human awareness and consciousness. Perhaps this primary life pattern, in affording an opportunity for the uninterrupted expression of the individual, offers a clue to the basic meaning of freedom, independence and equality, for the health and wholeness of man as a species implies the full and complete expression of the single organism.

But eons ago an unprecedented development took place. Through the modification of a segment of the forebrain, man was enabled to produce (at first unconsciously and later consciously) symbols or signs in substitution for actual objects or situations. There developed the faculty of language, through which men and women not only responded to the same thing with the same symbol, but through which they ultimately came to *know* that they responded in a like manner to the same thing. Through an unprecedented miracle of nature, our organism contrived to take the universe of its surroundings into itself, as it were, to incorporate it in its own neural tissues. A tree or a stream became a vocal sound. It became a spoken or a written word, and a mechanism emerged that related us to our universe of external matter and energy through a new system of receptivity and response. We now became related to the world of external objects and to one another through an entirely different system of neural reactions. (1964)[3]

With the beginning of the word a new adaptation set in—an adaptation that has not been appreciated in all its biological significance. From the background of our group experimentation it was seen that this adaptation did not consist only of a peripheral, socio-symbolic innovation, but that it has caused a radical modification in our organismic relation to one another as well as to the physical environment. We may assume that the inception of speech, or the shift upward of the function of communication to a special zone of the head, entailed at first but a slight somatic alteration. It probably began—and this again we see recapitulated in the immediate experience of ourselves and our children—as only a single sound or surface gesture here and there; and this sound or gesture corresponded to a single object or condition. Slowly, very slowly, the sounds and the gestures multiplied; and with this multiplication there occurred an altered awareness, an altered pattern of attention in respect to the objects and conditions for which the sounds and gestures stood.

Coincident with this local process or special modification in the cerebral area, reactions which hitherto had engaged the interest and elicited the emotive response of man's organism as a whole now also began gradually to be displaced upward. Thus it happened that with the descent of the generations, a tremendous behavioral transformation slowly took place. In the sphere of man's behavior as a social animal, the importance, interrelationally, of the whole organism began little by little to recede.

For with the acquisition by each of us of the facility of speech there resulted the social mechanism of agent and receptor. As occasion demanded, individuals could now stand to each other in the surface relation of subject and object. One might order, another obey; one might ask, another provide; one direct a task, another perform it. As men stood thus opposite one another, projecting words and observing the effect produced, something radical happened to the organism of man. There was the emergence of an altered interrelational function, a socially reciprocal adaptation among individuals that became more and more accentuated.

If now we may venture to reconstruct man's phylogenetic situation on the basis of our experiment in social groups, the inadvertent development which took place may be described somewhat as follows: With the increasing upward surge of the organism's emotive interests and drives, there was the centering of the individual's interrelational feeling and motivation in the anterior segment of the head and in the face. For with the enormous complexity and reorganization of function that arose coincidentally with the invention of language, there took place a special systematization within the brain and organism of man. With the upsurge of the emotive behavior of man and its amalgamation with his highly complex code of symbol usage, there developed a partitive behavior organization. In this systematization of man's subjective feelings and interests there was formed the restricted behavioral personality or identity I have called the "I"-persona.* (1950)[4]

As we know, man's bionomic relation to the world of objects is effected through the various superficial sense-organs occupying the periphery of his organism. It is through the medium of the periphery that the organism is related to the external world of phenomena. The peripheral senses which in man have come to be

* See pages 36–37.-Ed.

especially employed in mediating between his organism and the external world are the special exteroceptive senses located in the head, chiefly the visual and auditory senses. But these special sense-organs acquired secondarily a reciprocal action in their relation to one another and in their relation jointly to the muscles of phonation—chiefly those of the tongue, lips and larynx—which differentiated them sharply from their function in relation to the organism as a whole.* This circumscribed, partitive function, is analogous to the process which, in a different connection, has been described by Coghill as a partial reaction-pattern.** (1937)[5]

---

* Burrow later referred to this interfunctioning system as the "third nervous system" or "third brain" in contrast to the autonomic ("first") nervous system and the cerebrospinal ("second") nervous system. In describing the third nervous system" he wrote, "Basing this discrimination upon its topographical distribution to the special senses of vision and audition as well as to the muscles of the tongue and larynx, I demarcate a specially circumscribed area of neural function within the cranial segment . . . This 'third nervous system' is discriminated solely on the basis of its *specialization of function* within the organism's motivation as a whole. As with the two main divisions of the nervous anatomy—the cerebrospinal and the autonomic systems—so the system of nervous activation and response I have called the semiotic or symbolic system is delimited into a separate unit on grounds of its special physiological behavior . . . There is no rigid anatomical basis for this distinction . . . This third neural system is . . . demarcated from the other two on the strength of its special sociobiological function." (*The Neurosis of Man*, pp. 273–74)-Ed.

** From *The Biology of Human Conflict*, (pp. 275–76): In describing his studies of the neural growth of Amblystoma, Coghill in one of his papers briefly sums up the underlying principle of the organism's growth as "a progressive organization of the nervous system from the whole to the part." It should be repeated that, in accord with this principle of neural growth in animals, the behavior of the organism develops through the individuation of partial action-patterns or reflexes within a primary total action-pattern, and that this total pattern expands normally and from the beginning as an integrated process. Discrete reflexes or partial patterns are individuations arising out of and within this primary total pattern and, as Coghill repeatedly emphasizes, these secondary, restricted functions are dependencies under the jurisdiction of the total pattern. In a recent paper Coghill reviewed the findings of his study of Amblystoma and explained in addition that the mechanism of partial or secondary patterns, with their tendency toward independent autonomy, is essentially antagonistic to the mechanism of the total pattern. (Coghill, George E., "The Biologic Basis of Conflict in Behavior," *The Psychoanalytic Review*, 1933, pp. 1–4.)

The exaltation of one's prestige or *amour propre* has become bound up with and inseparable from our use of symbols, or our social interchange through speech. It marks a psychosocial process that tends to center or to focus chiefly in the interrelational reactions mediated by the head and face—the particular segment of the organism that subserves the function of symbol formation or language. The word "face" and the expression "saving of face" are, as we know, synonymous with one's sense of reputation, with prestige, with one's precious "right," indeed with one's very identity.

This self-enfoldment, this retroversion of the individual upon his own image has seriously dislocated processes that are basic in mediating man's relation to man. It has muddied the springs of native feeling and thinking and has distorted the primary coordination of man's organism as a species. (1949)[6]

With the segmentation of the species into the separate centers of interest and feeling that comprise each individual, there was correspondingly the separation, the opposition, the differentiation of individual interests from one another. The separate feeling of the individual was now the separate identity of the individual. Hence there was not only the objectively definable difference between agent and receptor, but man was now composed of *vicarious selves*, of artificially discrete identities. Personal sympathy or antipathy replaced man's primary empathy as a phylum, and we experienced a different *feeling relation* toward the environment and each other; interrelational conflict replaced the organism's coordination as a phylum. This is the breach whose global extension we see today in the irreconcilable ideologies of East and West.

Again, this development has its parallel in the child of today, the child that was once ourselves. In his first acquirement of words, no artificial division of the child's personality occurs; there is no behavioral conflict. It is only later—at the age of two or two and a half years—that separate feeling begins to be systematized into a separate identity,* and there are fashioned the divisive part-brain and the "I"-persona. It is at this stage that parents and educators speak of the child's "difficult age"—quite forgetting that their own difficult age still goes merrily on without check or hindrance. (1950)[7]

Among the observations which our group analysis early brought home to us with regard to the forces and relations determining the behavior of social man, the most important had to do with a deflection in the process of attention during the period of childhood. In man, as in other animals, the spontaneous education of the young in respect to the environment is a direct, biological function. Normally, the infant organism learns, or relates itself to its surroundings, through a consistent process of trial and error. It senses the differences between the soft and the hard object, between the hot and the cold. It distinguishes between the taste that is bitter and the taste that is sweet. In this and a thousand ways the infant comes to discriminate between the benign or fitting object or situation and the harmful or unfitting one. In a word, it develops a dependable sense of what is biologically right or true, and what is biologically wrong or false in relating it to the environment. In this process, through which the

---

* See Lewin, Kurt, "Environmental Forces," in Carl Murchison, ed. *A Handbook of Child Psychology* (2nd ed., Worcester, Mass.: Clark University Press, 1933, p. 619.)

infant familiarizes itself with the details of its surroundings, there is gradually established in the organism a *biological norm of behavior*. That is, the organism of the child acquires a *system* of relationships that
is objectively controlled or "intelligent," as we say.

In the course of its learning, the immature organism of man or animal is automatically assisted by the
parent whose learning has been acquired through a
like experience. In the genus man, however, the parent organism may further aid the child's discrimination between the true and the false response through
the use of words or symbols. The parent's encouragement or admonition through the use of the symbol may
greatly widen and augment the child's acquaintance
with the objects of its surroundings. It may greatly assist the child in differentiating between behavior that
is biologically right and behavior that is biologically
wrong.

But with the human parent this assistance to the
child's biological development has become seriously
interfered with. Too often a false, unstable norm is induced in the child through parental precepts of "right"
and "wrong" that are not supported by objectively ver-
ifiable experience. More often than not the behavior
prescribed by the parent is wholly at variance with a
biologically stable criterion. The instruction of the
child may derive from sheer traditional superstition or
belief. Or it may be motivated by personal considerations that are prompted solely by the parent's momentary convenience or wish.

In this wishful, prerogatory motivation of the parent—I am of course speaking, throughout, of the generic parent—a response is inculcated in the child that
is likewise unrelated to the objective environment.

Again, of course, I am speaking of the generic child, of the child that you and I once were. If the child, this generic child, conforms to what the mother says is "right," he wins love, approval and reward. If he does not conform, he incurs her ill will, rejection and punishment. Thus, where it is a question of the organism's social adaptation or its behavior, the infant generation is inducted into a purely wishful, nonobjective constellation of reactions to which there correspond only the *symbols* arbitrarily called "right" and "wrong." Wishing to be "right," wishing to be loved and approved, the child henceforth pursues a policy of *differential advantage* rather than one of cooperative and intelligent motivation. He is activated by partitive affects and prejudices rather than by basic feelings and emotions. The child—the child of the genus man—no longer adheres to a biological norm. His attention is diverted and henceforward he pursues a wishful pseudo-norm. There is thus in the genus man a biological rightness and an affect rightness.

As more and more our group or phylic analysis took us back to childhood, that is, as we returned in our generic analysis to our own generic childhood, we began to reach back to the origin of this esoteric mood of right and wrong and sense its meaning in our own lives. We saw that the "normal" parent does not convey to the infant a sense of behavior that is objectively right and behavior that is objectively wrong, the one to be cultivated, the other abjured. In his pseudo-normality the parent conveys only his or her subjective mood of differential advantage, the wishfully motivated mood of sovereign rightness. In other words, the ulterior, unilateral motivation of the parent generation induces an ulterior, unilateral motivation in the infant generation. In this way the parent generation makes of the infant generation mere passive *credulists* (if I may coin this term) rather than spontaneous investigators. This dissociation of man's organism from its continuity with the environment and with its kind through the induction of wishful, nonobjective reactions constitutes a *social dissociation or neurosis.**

In the process, then, whereby the child's feeling and thinking are derouted from their natural biological objectives toward the unreal goals of the parent, a change has been brought about in the primary function of the child's brain. In his wishful misadaptation, the dynamic function of the child's brain in its relation to the environment has undergone a marked physiological modification. This modification entails a phylobiological alteration. The brain of the growing child

---

* From "The Organismic Factor in Disorders of Behavior," pp. 335–36:

If I speak in one breath of the phenomenon of symbolic language and the phenomenon of behavior disorders, it must not be supposed that I am assuming any essential interdependence between these two incidents. It would be folly to attempt to trace in the coincidence of these two phenomena *per se* a relationship of cause and effect. Man's behavior disorders are without question his heaviest liability, while phonetic language is his outstanding asset. However, in the process of evolution, there may occur a conjunction between certain biological phenomena without the presence of an interdependence between them.

For example, early students of bacteriology noted the frequent coincidence of disease with certain sources of food or water supply. It was unthinkable that food could of itself be a source of disease. Water and food were too obviously the essential mainstays of the life and health of the organism. The idea, therefore, arose that possibly the cause of certain diseases was to be traced to some unrecognized agent associated with food and causing its contamination.

In the work of my associates and myself with disordered behavior reactions, as they occur in individuals and in groups, we were faced with an analogous problem. While obviously language could not of itself be held answerable for man's disorders of behavior, yet it did not seem excluded that indirectly language might be the vehicle of some pathogenic process. It did not seem excluded that there might be associated with man's adoption of language some agent or influence to which the existence of widespread behavior disorders within the species might be traceable.

has taken on an altered pattern of behavior.* This change in behavior involves the primary homeostasis of man's organism as a species. (1950)[8]

Of course the parent's wish or convenience is not without its place in the interrelational training of the child. Being maturer and more experienced, the parent may well voice wishes to which the child might profitably respond. It is only the unconscious, esoteric, unreasoning wish or motivation prevalent in "normality" that is the pedagogic rub. "Normally," differential advantage takes precedence over objective consistency. In parent, as in child, prejudice takes the place of thought; ulterior affect supplants inclusive feeling. This arbitrary and unconscious response is the deviation in attention on the part of parent and child to which I have referred as ditention.** (1949)[9]

It must not be thought that I wish to abrogate the use of symbols—that I have any desire to render man mute and inarticulate. Quite the contrary, my interest

---

* An exceptionally able article (Greenman, E. F. "The extraorganic." *Amer. Anthrop.*, 1948, 50, 181–99) discusses the principle of neurobiotaxis developed through the work of C. U. Ariëns, Kappers, C. Judson Herrick, Charles M. Child, J. B. S. Haldane, Julian Huxley and others. Greenman emphasizes the phenomenon of "projectilism" characterizing the behavior of man. He points out the "use-effect" in neurobiotaxis, or the way in which the employment of extraorganic implements (tools) may have played a decisive role in the development of the neural structure (brain) characteristic of the human species. Of special interest to us in the present communication, however, is the suggestion Greenman makes regarding the possible role played today by neurobiotaxis in relation to man's social behavior. To hazard a further elaboration of his thesis, it seems likely that extraorganic social manipulations, largely mediated through the function of language, could have brought about neurobiotactical rearrangements (especially in the association areas of the cortex) which are perpetuated from generation to generation by the type of social medium (culture) in which man lives. In this sense, one might speak of the neural substrate of man's behavior as being socially determined.

** The word *ditention* will be found in the Glossary.-Ed.

is precisely in man's greater facility in the use of this symbolic pattern of communication through his reintegrating it within the organism's primary pattern of behavior as a whole.* Although we are at this moment employing the symbol in our very effort to reckon internally with man's behavior in terms of internal physiological alterations, the symbol we are employing is merely an interindividual code and is therefore not primary as an agent for motivating and sustaining the organism's total behavior as a species. But due to the affect-coloring it has acquired, the symbol now represents an unrecognized process of social conditioning that has been induced within the phylum. This process, recapitulated ontogenetically in the nursery and at the family table, induces an interindividual pattern of behavior that now functions vicariously, verbally, as the dominant motivation of the organism's behavior as a whole. (1937)[10]

Life with us now is so much more a matter of adjusting the symbols that *represent* conduct than an expression of the biological processes that *are* conduct. We are so much more concerned with problems of understanding than with problems of behavior—with problems that attempt to cope with behavior as a mental picture or concept rather than with behavior itself. The accident that has split the feeling or interest of the integral social body into as many parts as there are individuals or groups of individuals composing

---

* From *Preconscious Foundations of Human Experience*, p. 109: The part-function of speech is of course a relatively recent acquisition and there are many indications that the species has not yet achieved the complete integration of this secondary part-function into the primary and sovereign function of the phyloorganism. This social part-function has been rendered independent of and even antagonistic to the primary behavior principle activating the organism of man as a species. (See fn. **, p. 61-Ed.)

the species, is but a temporary *faux pas*—a lapse of development in the course of our growth as conscious creative organisms. However prevalent, however powerful socially may be our sense of right as a sense of purely personal, private, segregated interests, there is within the race an equally powerful biological trend that makes for a healthy, whole and impartial adaptation among us. There is within man's physiological organism as a race a basic health or fitness that cannot be wholly extinguished—a health or fitness in contrast with which this external symbol called "right" with all its attending pathology may be recognized as a false and uneconomic substitution. (1937)[11]

One may perhaps ask, "Does phylobiology advocate depriving man of his rights?" If we are speaking of basic rights, the answer to this question is an emphatic "No." But one must add that the prerogatives that partitive individuals and communities call their "rights" are not their rights. They are presumptive claims that seriously interfere with the basic, prior rights of man's organism as a whole. Biologically, these lesser, these fugitive rights are not assets; they are liabilities. Through these partitive "rights" man as a species has been deprived of his primary unity—a unity that supersedes in importance all the transient claims, all the assumed prerogatives of every individual and of every group. Where the so-called rights of man entail a breach in the organism's primary function, these rights rest upon division and separation. The integrity of the organism of man, like the organism of other animals, rests on the primary solidarity and coordination of the species. The true rights of man are resident within his own tissues. (1949)[12]

In making a plea for studying man's behavior from

the basis of the organism's species solidarity, I am after all but returning to principles that form the accepted understructure of science. There is no organ of the body except the brain to whose function we bring an interpretation that is not based on the principle of phylic solidarity. We could not possibly treat disease or deviation of function in the liver or the lungs or the kidneys of various individuals of a species were we not aware that we are dealing with a phylically uniform and consistent structure.

Objectively, of course, I may know the liver, the heart or other bodily organs by reading about them in some book or dissecting them in an anatomical laboratory. Where it comes to a subjective knowledge of *my* organs, however; where it is a question of my own liver or heart or kidney as it functions within myself, I have no direct acquaintance with it. These organs are brought to subjective awareness only if there is *dis*comfort, *dis*order, *dis*ease.

So with the organ that is the brain of man. As with the kidney or the liver, under healthy, typical conditions, the brain functions automatically, imperceptibly. Man is unaware of the organ with which he is aware of all things else.

But with the organ that is the brain of man there is a difference—it makes direct contact with this same organ in other individuals. Its projective, interrelational function, thus relates the individual not only to the environment but also to other brains within the species man. It is this projective or interrelational function that I have specifically in mind at the moment. For, unlike the situation in respect to disfunction in the liver or kidney, even where there occurs interrelational partition or disfunction within the brain, man has no conscious recognition of this disturbance in brain-function. Though the organism's direct articulation with its surroundings is everywhere impaired; though man's interrelational behavior is shot through with habits of feeling and thinking that cause universal disturbance in communication interindividually and in respect to the environment; and though this factor is synonymous with ditentive adaptation, with "face," with *amour propre,* man does not sense the cerebral stress or pain that underlies this misadaptation. He does not recognize that these interrelational disorders are traceable to a disturbance in the interrelational or projective function of his own brain. It is highly expedient for us to look carefully into this circumstance. But to do so, we shall have to bring the matter closer home. We shall have to bring it back to ourselves in all its daily, subjective implications: My brain and that of my readers, performs its function in relation to the environment by virtue of the special process of mental projection. That is, in the functioning of our brain, the attention or interest is conveyed outward to the object envisioned. But, as I have said, there has occurred functional impairment or disorder in the use of this brain, yours and mine, and because of our preoccupation with the external object or condition which we project and in which we have come to be wholly absorbed, we do not become aware of a disorder or impairment of function within this organ that is our own brain.

Thus partitive feeling, or affect, has seriously distorted the subjective function of our brain. To illustrate: in my substitution of a partitive premise of motivation, I may say that a person who is harshly critical of me offends me, causes me pain, whereas the real occasion of my pain or offense is my organism's lack of balance or integration. The brain is led to false and unwarranted perceptions or inferences, and, because this ditentive pattern of reaction now involves my whole organism (man's whole organism), instead of seeking a remedy for my deviation or disfunction I tend (man tends) to contribute further to my difficulty by falsely ascribing my brain's inharmonious functioning to the circumstances or person on whom my interest is projected. (1949)[13]

This illusory mechanism is the meaning of the affect-anomaly I enact when I "see" a person as other than myself in the sense of his being organically discontinuous from and opposite to me. It is this inept racial habit that is answerable for the organic illusion of the "transference," as it is answerable for its "conscious" recall in systems of psychotherapy designed to bring about a patient's social readjustment. The practical result of this affect-habit is one that is seriously subversive of the individual's harmonious activity, as it is subversive of the interactivity of individuals composing the species as a whole.

Thus I "see," or believe I "see," a face as fitting to be kissed or punched as the case may be. I see an object or person as worthy to be owned or not to be owned, and the merit or demerit assigned in either instance I ascribe to the object or condition which I "see." I do not deal with my feeling-reaction as something within my own organism that has been artificially projected upon an object or person. (1937)[14]

In consequence, there is disorder and pain. But, unlike disfunction in the stomach or kidney, disorder in the interrelational function of the brain of man is not experienced as pain in the brain. Just as man projects everything else in his use of the brain, so in his use of the brain he also projects his own pain. Moreover, the pain and disorder due to a deviation in the function of man's brain constitutes a social as well as an individual anomaly. Man's conflict and pain entails a social neurosis—a phyloneurosis which, though universal, is still projected outward and man is still at war with man, still at war with himself, whether in peace or in war. (1949)[15]

What we have most to keep in mind, it seems to me—to keep in our *feeling* would better say what I mean—is the all-encompassing nature of our conflict and neurosis. We need to make this phylic feeling so real, to bring it so close home to us that there can be no room for any division, for any discrimination in our condition as a species. The discrete, private ache—the ache that seems so engrossing to any phylically isolated you or me—is just another misappropriation on the part of the "I"-persona. The ache is really man's, not the ache of any separate you or me; just as the "I"-persona is an appropriation on the part of social (affecto-symbolic) man, and does not indict any individual or group of individuals as we, in our divisive "wrongness," like to "think." Organismically, or in the phylobiological reckoning, you and I are man too, just as any nonplussed Dmitri behind *his* iron curtain of affect is also man, and shares with us in this ache that is man's. This basis of feeling and thinking, however, depends upon our foregoing an habitual brain-function based upon differentiation and projection, and recovering a pattern of reaction that is integrated and unitary. As I shall attempt to show, it depends upon the discipline of converting "impacted" affect into the sensation of neuromuscular stress that underlies it. (1953)[16]

In the broader medical premise of phylobiology

we must regard the symptoms embodied in interrelational disorders or neurosis as the expression of a basic *intra*relational disfunction. When I speak of such a disorder I have in mind a condition of disturbed tension that affects the organism's relation to the environment and to others of the species. I have in mind a condition of stress or tension that is as yet unrecognized and that affects the organism's bionomic function. What is habitually called one's transference—one's love, anger, dependence or disaffection, his competitiveness or superiority in respect to someone else—is a quite superficial interpretation. Man's real disturbance is a physiological conflict, a disorder in intrarelational function that dislocates the organism's basic homeostasis—its balanced relationship to the environment and to others.

Where we come to deal with the biological process that regulates the interrelational behavior of man, the functional norm required to be established is the norm that governs man's internal processes of feeling and thinking in relation to the external environment, and the feeling and thinking of individuals and communities in their relation to one another. This norm of behavior which concerns man's attentional or adaptive processes is the pattern of behavior I have called *cotention*. Cotention is an expression of the phyloorganism's primary motivation.

It is synonymous with the solidarity of the species. Like the criteria of health established by medical science in regard to bodily structures, cotention also is a criterion of health. But there is a difference. Cotention represents healthy, in contrast to unhealthy, behavior-reactions *within the field of man's interrelations*.

In the sphere of man's interrelational adaptation,

the criteria of cotention are sharply contrasted with manifestations of *ditention* or with man's partitive, autopathic feeling and thinking.* A person with typhoid fever is restored to health when the typhoid germ has been eliminated from his organism and he presents no further symptoms occasioned by this bacterial infection. So with the organism's interrelational health. The healthy, cotentive adaptation of man is automatically present when the intrusion of ditentive elements has been intercepted.

Again, to compare our position with that of the physician who deals with structural disease occurring in the individual, if we are to restore man's healthy interrelational processes, it is necessary that we discount the external symptoms of his interrelational disorder and examine into the underlying functions responsible for these outer manifestations.

The phylobiologist, like the internist, must also look deeper than mere symptoms. The social symptoms of hate, disdain, antagonism, crime and war; the symptoms evidenced in the sense of guilt, fear, repression and violence; and the complemental symptoms of transference with their clinging dependence, their nostalgias and sentimentalities; in short, the symptoms of partition characterizing the social neurosis are, like the symptoms of the individual patient, but superficial manifestations. They are like the fever or prostration of the malarial or tubercular patient, or of a community of patients. Like these diseases, the interrelational disorders of man are not diagnosed and treated by translating them into words and

---

* The terms *cotention, ditention* and *autopathic* are listed in the Glossary.-Ed.

symbols. Conversational therapy, whether interpersonal or group, does not touch the problem of man's neurodynamic dislocation in relation to the environment. This phylic dislocation has entered too deep into the physiology of man's daily life. In this hour it is ravaging the very tissues of man. The phylobiologist must demand to know the *neurology* of behavior-disorders, both individual and social. But he must demand to know the neurology of these disorders internally, organismically, or as *reactions perceptible within himself.*

It is the mark of science that it recognizes the element as a complete and integral expression of the total structure of which it is an elemental part. In short, science always sees in the part or element the potential structure and function of the whole, whether healthy or diseased. And as a scientist, man has not departed from this principle of observation and study in respect to the structure and function of his own organism. But this principle requires to be applied to the *behavior* of man, to the motivation or function of man as a phylum. Only on this basis may we study deviations of function occurring in the wider social community, and measure them in relation to a biological norm or in relation to man's cotentive solidarity as a species. (1949)[17]

Source Notes

1 "Prescription for Peace," pp. 94–96
2 *Preconscious Foundations of Human Experience,* pp. 103–04
3 *Ibid.,* pp. 105–07
4 "Prescription for Peace," pp. 96–98
5 *The Biology of Human Conflict,* pp. 150–51
6 *The Neurosis of Man,* pp. 40, 42
7 "Prescription for Peace," pp. 99–100
8 "Emotion and the Social Crisis," pp. 470–76
9 "Two Modes of Social Adaptation and Their Concomitants in Ocular Movements," p. 193
10 *The Biology of Human Conflict,* pp. 256–57
11 *Ibid.,* pp. 63–64
12 *The Neurosis of Man,* p. 336
13 *Ibid.,* pp. 194–97
14 *The Biology of Human Conflict,* pp. 228–29
15 *The Neurosis of Man,* p. 198
16 *Science and Man's Behavior,* pp. 67–68
17 *The Neurosis of Man,* pp. 190–94

IV

The "How" of Attention

Editor's Note

This chapter is concerned with ways to sense the internal, somatic basis of the human dilemma, as defined by Burrow. He states the problem in terms of a disturbance in the function of attention—attention viewed in its broad sense as the physiological process that links us to the environment. In the preceding chapter reference was made to the contrasting modes of attention Burrow distinguished as cotention *and* ditention. *Readers will already be aware that di-tention represents divided attention, diverted by the affective self-image.* Co-tention *(attention* with*) is the mode of organismic wholeness, the common tension of the organism, individual and phylic.*

Steps were developed by Burrow and his associates to interrupt the dominance of ditention and the "I"-persona and to reestablish cotention, at least experimentally.* These steps were first described in 1935 in Burrow's paper "Neuropathology and the Internal Environment." Since then, the practice of meditation has become familiar in Western countries

---

* Instrumental evidence of this shift of attention is discussed in Chapter V.-Ed.

and, thanks in part to Burrow's studies, the number of somatic approaches to problems of behavor adjustment have increased. Many people will see similarities between Burrow's phylobiological procedures and certain forms of meditative and somatizing disciplines.

The limits of my own experience with these disciplines precludes adequate comparisons—others will doubtless make them in time. Burrow himself did not relate his technique in any way to traditional religious, philosophical or mystical approaches; he characterized it as prosaic and pragmatic—concerned, not with "spiritual meanings," but with the "quite simple physiological appreciation" of the total organism (p. 97).

In connection with this practice, readers will find that the word affect *appears more frequently in the ensuing chapters to designate the partisan, self-biased mood of what Burrow called the "normal reaction-average." This distorting affect mood of personal rightness and prerogative has been identified in previous chapters with the "I"-persona and ditention.*

This chapter also introduces the terms ontosoma *and* phylosoma. *They describe the human organism as individual and as species respectively, and emphasize the biological grounding of our interrelational life.*

The problem of human relations is a problem in attention. The process of attention is a physiological process that relates the organism to the objects about it. Words, opinions, ideas are the outer signs of a specialized and selective part of this physiological process—the part which serves us in naming or identifying the objects or processes about us. On the other hand, the impetus to attention subjectively experienced as interest or feeling, as it relates the organism to the total object or condition about it, is a socio-physiological reaction involving the functional activity of the organism as a whole. (1932)[1]

Attention is all but synonomous with the relation of an organism to its environment. Attention is thus an essentially bionomic or ecological process. Without attention there would be no contact with the outer world. There would not be man's apprehension of the objects and conditions that surround him. There would not be his ecosomatic or organism-environment relationship.* And so, in looking for a clue to the processes that determine man's behavior, we cannot do better than devote ourselves to a consideration of the function of attention as it links together organism and environment. (1949)[2]

Attention has come to mean for us only the function we habitually experience when focusing "mentally" upon this or that object or image of an object. The sharply directive pencil or focus of interest with which we apply ourselves mentally to a specific object or phenomenon constitutes an example of what is for

---

*The phrase *organism-environment* relationship seems a bit awkward so that I propose the adoption of the handier term *ecosomatic* relationship (οἶκος = environment, σῶμα = organism) in discussing the broader aspects of man's bionomic adaptation.

us now practically the sum of the process understood as "attention." This mental penciling upon an item, whether actual object or retained image, is however, from the point of view of man's evolution, a very recent and specialized acquisition. The process of attention originally represented far more a coordination of the organism *with* the object than a directing of its interest *at* the object. (1937)[3]

We need more and more to bring home to us that the meaning of attention is adaptation, that it means man's relation to the objects about him and the employment of these objects in the service of those needs which contribute to his maintenance and survival as an individual and as a race. Thus adaptation or attention is essentially industrial. It is the industry of the organism as a whole in its application to the environment as a whole. (1932)[4]

Impaired attention is unbalanced behavior, for attention is ourselves in action. It is the physiology of our organisms reacting towards and in response to the physical objects of the outer world. As the function of attention mediates between the brain and the environment, it seemed to me that this was the field to which one must look for an understanding of man's interrelational behavior and its disorders. (1949)[5]

Primarily the "I"-persona is a defect in the process of attention and the adjustment of this defect is our basic problem. Let us turn, then, to ourselves. Let us turn to the ontogenetic (individual) aspect of this biological transformation as it influences the behavior of social groups today. This accident in man's development is, as we have said, a subjective accident. It is an accident that has befallen you and me. Hence unless we return to ourselves—unless we appreciate this accident within our own subjective processes as we live and have our being today in a society of artificial personality structures—we shall not be in a position to reckon objectively and to remedy effectively this subjective defect in our own socio-symbolic* evolution. (1950)[6]

So let us return to the contrasting patterns of attention and motivation (cotention and ditention) to which I have alluded as constituting the underlying physiology of the symptoms we enact under the sponsorship of a spurious normality. Let us consider the tensions which upon physical diagnosis we find to be concomitant to man's phylic dislocations in behavior. For we are now dealing with the very fine discrimination between the function that mediates man's socio-symbolic capacity of interchange and the function that mediates the adaptation of man's total organism both to his physical and his social environment. The perception of this delicate differentiation in neuromuscular adjustment is essential, but it is not easy. The displacing of the ditentive in favor of the cotentive pattern of behavior is not an adjustment to be blithely achieved.

If, however, through the ingenuity of the total organism, the agitated "I"-persona may be induced to hold still long enough to allay the go-getting drives of self-interest and competitiveness that now obtrude upon the interrelational sphere, we may materially assist the reestablishment of the tensions belonging to man's basic pattern of motivation. Through the suitable technique one may perceive within his own organism the difference between the pattern of tension that pertains to the symbolic segment of the brain with

---

* Social interchange by means of symbol and speech. See Glossary.-Ed.

its partitive affects and prejudices (ditention), and the pattern of tension that pertains to the primary nervous system and that is consonant with man's total biological behavior in relation to the environment (cotention). Thus, we may distinguish between a pattern of tension that has artificially disintegrated the behavior of the species in its primary motivation,* and a pattern of tension that integrates the behavior of man in its organismic solidarity. (1949)[7]

Because of its central position functionally between the organism's exteroceptive action-pattern and its proprioceptive pattern of response, the organ of vision constitutes physiologically an organic integral that is common to both these systems. One would expect, therefore, that this organ common to the two systems would be especially disposed to register whatever conflict or overlapping of function has been induced through a disparity of tensions between them. As we are well aware, even if a very small element is an integral part of a pattern-complex, the stimulation of this element is sufficient to excite a reaction throughout the entire pattern. It is therefore not extravagant to expect that if we might modify the reaction of this integral element, however small, we should be able to modify also the reaction of the pattern-complex in which it is a functioning component.

As a matter of fact, one finds through actual internal observation that the organ of vision and its adjacent

---

* From "The Organismic Factor in Disorders of Behavior," 1937, pp. 336–37: The partitive tensions which in man are associated with language or the symbol were found to coexist equally with the organism's benign as with its antagonistic behavior expressions. These unassimilable tensions were found to be present no less in compliance than in irritability, and they were found equally in the contrasting phases of elation and depression occurring in normal and abnormal states.

structures afford a significant clue in the effort to give sharper outline to the sensation of overlapping and conflict existing between these two reaction-patterns. In the contradictory and quite irreconcilable sensations of strain that coalesce at this point of juxtaposition one finds a valuable entering wedge to the internal physiological conflict between them. The tensions of the eye in orienting the organism in respect to the environment symbolically or partitively possess a wholly different character from the tensions of the eye when responding as an element within a total system of kinesthetic balance and coordination. While these two types of eye-tension differ from one another, each type is, of course consistent within its own domain. Between these two types of visual reaction there exists no essential conflict—not any more than the movements performed by the tongue or lower jaw in speech interfere or conflict with their function in the process of digestion. Interference occurs only as the partial action-pattern belonging to the symbolic or partitive segment tends to reverse the primary behavior of the organism by dominating the total behavior-system to which it is subordinate. Under these conditions the organ of vision registers strain and discomfort because of its function as a common organic integral in these two conflicting behavior systems. (1937)[8]

In the effort to differentiate the two physiological patterns (cotention and ditention), the tensions in the region of the eyes were at first our only index. They were, however, an unfailing index because of the key position the eyes occupy, as I have indicated, in relation both to the organism's partitive or reflexly induced behavior-pattern and to its primary or central pattern of behavior. They were an index because man's socially ambivalent images are, according to our finding, concomitant to an internal physiological alteration. This alteration consists in the circumstance that the tensions in the ocular musculature have become dissociated from the organism's center of control or from its internal system of tensions as a whole. In other words we found ourselves making direct contact with the neuromuscular substrate of man's conditioned pattern of attention. This development gave the first indication of the neurodynamic* basis underlying the indirect, haphazard system of ditentive responses that now replaces the phyloorganism's cotentive pattern of reaction as a whole.

It was this unique finding, based upon repeated experimentation, that brought to evidence the existence in this area of a subjectively appreciable pattern of stress or tension—a pattern of stress or tension due, doubtless, to our conscious arrest of a partitive behavior-reaction grown habitual to the organism.

At first this sense of stress or of internal shear, so to speak, was only of sporadic occurrence and stubbornly eluded all efforts to recapture it at will. But gradually the tension in the cephalic segment grew to be more frequent and more pronounced, until finally, after long-repeated experimentation, it was possible to elicit this localized tension at any moment. As the pattern of tension associated with ditention is connected with a specific type of eye-behavior, the procedure which seemed at first of greatest assistance in getting in touch with this localized partitive pattern was that of sensing the pattern of tension in the region of the eyes. It consisted in differentiating this localized pattern from the organism's pattern of tension as a whole.

---

* Listed in the Glossary.-Ed.

In doing so, one automatically intercepts not only the images concomitant to the oculomotor tensions, but also whatever affects are linked with them.

The first step in the method followed by my associates and myself consisted in closing the eyes. While in one's attempt to restore cotention the eyes need not necessarily be closed, it seemed helpful, at least in the beginning, to employ this procedure. With the eyes closed and with only the sense of complete darkness before them, our aim was to maintain a steadfast internal sense of the balance and tension connected with the eyes. In my own case, the effort, as I looked at the curtain of uniform blackness, as it were, before me, was to rest the eyes on the point (not visible of course) that was felt kinesthetically to be directly in line with the normal visual axis. That was all. This "all," however, consisted, in fact, in the sustained awareness of an indeterminate physiological process subjectively appreciable by the organism.

Where it was possible to sustain this posture over any considerable period of time (such a period amounted in the beginning to a few seconds only), the elimination of customary affect-images took place automatically. The mental and emotional pain and disappointment resultant from the frustration among us of ditentive social feelings and impulses was suddenly dissipated. If imagery occurred, it was of a different quality or character from that which prevails in the field of man's customary social images.

This altered mode represented a reaction that could be quite clearly differentiated from the mode accompanying the affect-stimulation and self-concern of ordinary social interchange (ditention). In general, I would say that the cotentive mode of feeling and

thinking was characterized by a constructive, impersonal type of interest that is inclusive or organismic.
While our experiment in the field of mental and emotional reactions was at that time only tentative, it
seemed to us even then that the alteration in the individual's reaction in response to the discipline of group
frustration consisted in a shift to a basis of motivation
that is primary and organismic. (1949)[9]

As this sensation of stress became more clearly defined within the anterior portion of the head, there was
the coincident awareness of an altered tensional tone
distributed generally throughout the body. This altered tensional pattern appeared to constitute a background or foil, so to speak, against which the localized
pattern stood out in sharp relief.

It should be emphasized, however, that in so far as
the posture of the eyes was maintained, it was maintained from a purely kinesthetic sense of the eyes and
their muscular appendages. Even where cotention
was induced with open eyes it was necessary that their
fixation be preserved through an internal balance in
muscular tone and not through fixation on some external point. (1941)[10]

Of special interest to our experimental group was
the circumstance mentioned earlier that symbolically
induced reactions—ambivalent mental images and the
dichotomous motivations accompanying them—were
automatically excluded so long as the balanced position of the eyes was maintained through the organism's internal control of the ocular muscles. In the
initial stage of the experiment, the attainment of this
internal muscular balance of the eyes was, as already
indicated, an indispensable prerequisite in differentiating the organism's primary cotentive balance of

function from the partitive ditentive pattern of function.

It was our finding that, unlike the sense of ease present in any other coordinated group of muscles in a state of rest, complete relaxation of the oculomotor system of muscles does not exist at any time (unless, perhaps, in profound sleep), nor may relaxation of these muscles be induced at will. Even under conditions most favorable to quiet and repose, there still persists a feeling of stress or tension as one directly observes, or becomes aware of, the eyes. As our experiments continued, the perception of this tension became a matter of routine in controlling the organism's external adaptation. In other words, this physiological tension in the forepart of the head became immediately appreciable as belonging to the plane of partitive reactions associated with the "I"-persona, with man's "right-wrong" behavior-dichotomy as contrasted with the homeostatic balance of tensions that relates the organism primarily to the environment.

Henceforward, then, the efforts of my associates and myself in maintaining the organism's balanced behavior were directed toward a consistent discrimination between two neuromuscular systems of tension—between the organism's partitive pattern of tension and its primary pattern of tension. The first or partitive mode of reaction is concomitant to ditention or to the organism's socially conditioned excitations; the second or organismic mode of reaction is concomitant to the total unconditioned type of adaptation I have already described as cotention. (1949)[11]

My own procedure has been to set aside during the day (and night) experimental periods in which I have adhered so consistently to the arrest of the eyes and the concomitant kinesthetic observation of the cephalic area of partitive tension that the background from which it is observed, namely, the organism's primary tensional pattern, or cotention, is forced into recognition and into conscious, directive efficiency. That is, the technique for bringing into operation the pattern of cotention, or the tensional pattern of the organism as a whole, consists in centering upon the part-area of discomfort and stress, with the resultant arrest of affect images. (1950)[12]

But it should be emphasized that our investigation of internal strains and tensions does not concern itself primarily with these internal manifestations as they become perceptible in this or that particular neuromuscular segment or body-part. They are concerned with subjectively perceptible tensions as they are related to the behavior of the organism as a whole. It is then upon the imbalance of the internal tensions belonging to the two differentiated systems of response—the total systemic reaction or cotention, and the partial, symbolic reaction or ditention—that my associates and I have been led to concentrate our investigations. (1937)[13]

To suppose, then, that a mere discrimination in ocular tensions is the solution of man's disorders of adaptation, individual and social, is to presume a facility in total kinesthetic adjustment that is quite fantastic. What is required is a consistent internal appreciation of the system of tensions that constitute the basic and prior motivation of the organism (cotention) as they contrast with tensional patterns that are concomitant to one's habitually partial, externally conditioned reflexes (ditention). This restitution of pat-

terns existing within us *en masse* implies an un-
equivocal assault upon one's most cherished, one's
most deeply conditioned affects or biases. It is to arrest
reflexes which have dominated the behavior of the organism from earliest childhood and which have come
to enjoy the automatic support of the social community. It is possible, however, as I have indicated throughout these pages, for students of behavior to undertake
such an intra-organic investigation based upon the evidence of immediate sensation (1937)[14]

Because of man's subjective bias in favor of his
habitually conditioned affects, the discrimination of
this line of differentiation is far easier in theory than in
practice. The long-continued subordination of the investigator himself to personal bias or to his own systematization of affects makes it extremely difficult for
him to keep consistently in mind the internal and, at
the same time, objective nature of his problem. For,
though the problem is internal to himself, it is no less
physiological and objective than problems presented
in other medical fields. The fact is, the student is faced
with an immediate and exacting problem in internal or-
thopedics. There is, however, a further difficulty. This
difficulty consists in the extreme delicacy of the line of
demarcation between the two tensional patterns—a
line that entails a functional distinction which may be
compared with the fine histological discrimination the
early students of bacteriology were required to make
in attempting to "recognize" a microorganism they
had never before seen and of which, therefore, they
had no preexistent image or model.

The reader will, of course, realize that this broader
premise of behavior was not achieved overnight. As a
matter of fact our research group worked steadily over

many years before attaining a consistent sense of this
more basic behavioral pattern. While, in looking back,
one may relate this experience in a few lines, the research itself covered many years of experimentation
and was fraught with many errors in procedure and
with many impediments and delays. For, simple and
natural as is the primary cotentive pattern, the habit of
adhering reflexly to the secondary pattern of ditention
makes difficult the recapture of the primary adapta-
tional mode. (1949)[15]

Before going further we may well consider certain
broad generalizations. The reader will have seen that
cotention means integration, coordination or health;
and that ditention means disintegration, disorder or
disease. Cotention is basic or primary. Just as the bony
skeleton is the organism's structural framework, so cotention is the organism's functional support. It is the
individual's balance wheel; it is the homeostat of organismic man. Ditention, on the other hand, is always
secondary and always indicates a shift from the organism's primary matrix of cotention to an over-em-
phasis upon some special part or part-function of the
individual, with resulting tensional imbalance.

In all stages of learning or of adaptation to one's
environment from childhood on, the functional behavior of the single organism is invariably cotentive,
unless ditention has intervened. Each new adaptation
of whatever sort begins with a relatively difficult, awkward stage during which there is always the latent possibility of ditentive intervention, and ends with the
functionally satisfying and pleasurable achievement of
cotentive balance. Once the cotentive adaptation has
been completed, it sticks; it has become an inseparable part of the organism's balanced, healthy equip-

ment. It has become an integral part of the total functioning organism. For instance, the expert surgeon is completely oblivious of the intricate, delicate, yet ever assured and balanced performance of his senses and his body-musculature while he is performing an operation. This is as it should be. This is healthy, balanced, cotentive function.

There is, however, the circumstance that where there is present a curvature of the spine, here too, notwithstanding that the curvature represents a definite maladaptation, one may be quite unaware of it. But we must bear in mind that in such a maladaptation there is, in general, a trend that directly or indirectly predisposes the organism to disease. In instances of this kind in which one tends to forget the maladaptation, we need also bear in mind that the powerful, primary, adaptable cotentive pattern of function of the organism as a whole is ever at work in furthering the most favorable adjustment in spite of ditentive handicaps.

These general observations in respect to cotention and ditention apply throughout the life of man in both the ontosoma and the phylosoma.* Just as there are functional disorders in the individual organism so throughout the phylum man we may become so accustomed to disordered and diseased behavioral ways of living that we take them for granted; as I have pointed out, we even regard these disorders as normal. I am now referring, of course, to man's broad, socially systematized field of disbehavior generally. As far as concerns human behavior, man is still in the stumbling stage of his development. Painfully beset with unreal and undependable images, he is naively whistling in

---

* Listed in the Glossary.-Ed.

the dark, feverishly rushing about, trying to cure this symptom or that with one palliative after another.

There is no doubt that in time man will bring his scatterbrained behavior under the sovereignty of his total phylic organism. Sooner or later he will recognize the physiologically common tensional disorder from which his present interrelational confusion arises. For the organism of man, like the individual organism, was originally and primarily patterned not for disease, neurosis and war, but for health, for whole organismic functioning throughout the species. (1949)[16]

*It is strange how insulated we have all come to feel toward one another. We could not possibly doubt—not any of us—the oneness and continuity of the social structure that unites us symbolically as people of a common language and meaning. We accept without question the common tie of "meaning." But beneath meaning and before meaning ever was, there was the structure out of which all our meaning has been fashioned—the common bodily structure and function that have given us the building-material of all our symbols, all our common implements of understanding and social contact.

In a sense there isn't depression, there isn't even conflict. Where tissues are torn apart, there is pain—inevitably pain. We just haven't yet thought of *man's* unity and continuity in terms of organically inseparable tissues and functions. In our restriction to the lens of the personal and partitive we know division only of *the* man—the man that is I, or that through some process of inner identification may be felt as *if* I (love, sympathy, possession, etc.). And we have not sensed

---

* From a letter to William E. Galt.

that this lens that has led to our false perceptions, and to feelings that are correspondingly false, has been fashioned within and *of* our own common tissue, that we must return to this common tissue within us if we are to correct our common error of vision and of feeling. This is the philosophy of integration. The philosophy. But integration (cotention) isn't philosophy. Not any more than a surgical operation is philosophy. Like surgery, integration* is the reuniting of tissues that have been torn apart. If the process is not accomplished with sutures, it is nevertheless a process of suturing. It is the restoration of an organismic commissure that has been artificially severed.

Your pain, *my* pain, then, is the way each of us artificially looks at the pain of man through the division that is precisely you and me. A manner of healing, though, is definitely in process among us, and therefore, being organismic, among the race of man.

I think we have not yet approached our thesis from a sufficiently broad, organismic (internal) frame of reference. Our approach to a partitive deviation is itself partitive. We still attempt to negotiate an adjustment that is non-partitive, the while we maintain a basis that is partitive, psychic, imaginal—socio-imaginal, of course. It won't work. It is self-preclusive. "Integration" is precisely the indispensable bridge from the insular position man has artificially adopted to the mainland of his organism as a whole. The bridge is exceedingly narrow, but it is also exceedingly short. To cross it calls for delicate balance apparently, but it must be crossed and by a route that is physiological.

---

* Integration refers to the procedure which Burrow later called the phylobiological or cotentive technique (described on pp. 85–90 and elsewhere).-Ed.

With constant, careful and delicate probing you'll inevitably come upon the tiny fasciculus of "reference" that will more and more firmly conduct you to the mainland of feeling and motivation that was the birthplace of man. It is not proceeding in the direction of the organism's mainland to seek a partitive mitigation of a partitive disorder, such as we do when we revert from the seemingly personal insulation of "depression" to the merely socially anesthetizing sense of continuity we have in "elation." That is to miss the interconnecting causeway to the mainland—the commissure or connecting fasciculus between the "psychic" and the organismic.

The clue undoubtedly lies in the sensation of the eyes themselves rather than in the habitual sensation of the images "projected" by the eyes. Reflexes and habituations are the physiological substrate of the operation we know or rather experience as wishes. The wish will not be gainsaid by wishing. That, as I said, is self-preclusive. The steadied eye, however, makes connection, albeit an infinitesimal connection, with a pattern that affords a basis of contrast with the wishful (the psychic or reflexly habitual) mode of adaptation, and this nuance of contrast provides the organism with the requisite fulcrum for overthrowing the wishfully superimposed dominance of the socially insular *I*. (1938)[17]

The technique of working with physiological tensions is not, as some students think, a handy recourse for furthering one's personal comfort or convenience. In fact, in first working with the tensional patterns of the organism that underlie behavior, one finds the task uninteresting and difficult. All the customary incentives are for not continuing with the somatic discipline. But whatever the difficulties, we really must become internally acquainted with the cotentive pattern—not my cotention, or yours, but man's; not now and again, but as the permanent reinstatement of an intraorganismic configuration. The physiological pattern of cotention, when it becomes a *fait accompli*, entails a fundamental alteration in one's basis of motivation, in one's very center of identity. (1953)[18]

But if anyone supposes that to attain the pattern of cotention is to attain a state of Nirvana, that with the discovery of this pattern he has come into possession of "spiritual meanings" hitherto undreamed of in the philosophies, that he is about to adopt some manner of Yogi practice or experience something akin to the beatific vision of the mystics, let him be warned that his trend is definitely away from his biological base, not back to it. None of these comforting self-propitiations play any part in man's quite simple physiological appreciation of the function of his own organism as a total entity.

On the contrary, in approaching cotention the organism finds itself upon quite prosaic, pragmatic ground. The problem is really a simple one. Perhaps an analogy may be found in the altered pattern one must attain on learning to swim. To one who does not know how to swim, the water is a quite alien medium, and he invariably sets out to make its acquaintance along lines of his habitual reaction to the solid ground—a reaction precisely contrary to the behavior required of the swimmer. Where one is on *terra firma* and there is question of his security, of his footing, he seeks automatically for a more solid base. His tendency is to grab for something that will help sustain his poise. So it is at first with the venturer into the un-

familiar medium of water. With the very first threat to
his accustomed balance, his reaction is a frantic effort
to secure a firmer hold. His impulse is to grab. But his
grabbing is in fact the most inappropriate response he
could make. What is needed is that he let go of his
usual physiological pattern of security and, instead,
make use of a different pattern—a pattern adjusted to
his altered environment. For he must exchange a solid
for a fluid medium of security, and the organism must
entrust itself completely to the support of this new
menstruum.

On land, of course, the organism supports itself
through the proper adjustment of the external skeletal
muscles, or through the appropriate adjustment of the
body's tensions in relation to its surroundings. But in
maintaining its balanced support in the water, one's
security is dependent upon air-intake, and one needs
to place full confidence in the ability of the organism
to support itself with this aim in view. The swimmer
must, on entering the water, adopt a pattern that depends upon the balanced pliancy of his internal respiratory and general motor adjustment to the altered
medium. In this way he finally learns to swim.

Needless to say, a person does not ordinarily give
himself airs on learning to swim—not any more than on
learning to walk. On acquiring the facility to swim,
marked as this departure is from his habituations on
land, he does not feel he has attained the millennium.
Adopting the requisite pattern of balance, he quite
simply swims, and there is no more to it. After all, as
the evolutionists have taught us, man was an aquatic
animal many eons before land became his natural
habitat. Similarly, with respect to man's internal behavior: the pattern of cotention antedated the pattern

of ditention by countless thousands of years, and to reestablish this original pattern, so long forgotten, presents little occasion for special pride or affectation. To be anything but cotentive is to be deviate, dissociative; it is not to be one's bionomic self. Surely to be merely what one is, is not an achievement to be signalized with a fanfare of trumpets.

In comparing swimming with cotention, I am resorting, as I said, to mere analogy. Nevertheless, the two reactions possess certain common features. Under the dominion of ditention or of affect-images one is ever grabbing on behalf of the "I"-persona. We are ever grabbing for the fleeting image of our preeminent "right." One must somehow preserve a policy of unilateralism. Such is the ditentive pattern of behavior with its short, quick staccato movements ever alert for this and that interrelational advantage or opportunity. In this mechanism the organism's spontaneous grasp reflex has been transformed into a sophisticated and monopolistic grab reflex.

With the pattern of cotention, on the other hand, motivation arises from the internal need and interest of the organism. In cotention one assimilates from the environment; one does not grab but reacts spontaneously to the organism's need. Though effortless, cotention is productive. In the cotentive pattern one seeks only what is his own organismically, and seeks it only by reason of the natural interest of the object in relation to one's own capacity or endowment.

Ditention rests upon a subjective, unilateral interpretation of behavior; cotention on an interpretation which, being organismic, is consistently objective and inclusive. Cotention is synonymous with functional balance, organismically and intraorganismically. It is identified with ease, quiet, clarity, and preparedness, both in feeling and in thought. Cotention is a function that is free and capacious. It is steadfast and dependable both in normal function and in emergency. Cotention deplores the partitive step before taking it. It crosses the bridge before coming to it.

With the reestablishment of cotention and the reintegration of organism with environment, the necessity to struggle, to leap for this and that advantage in competition with others, falls away. From now on the outlook becomes broad, impersonal, affirmative. The spirit of disinterested research, and with it the disinterested spirit of living and letting live, now takes precedence over a fancied prerogative of affectivity and unilateralism. With the attainment of this altered mode, the student automatically begins to function as man, to think and feel as man, to recover his organism's basic primacy and with it the experience of a full and mature consciousness. He begins to sense the basic principle of his organism's motivation before there was inculcated a sense of "I"—the social image of separateness, of distinction, of private and personal importance. He begins to transmute into terms of consciousness the undifferentiated preconscious mode of behavior that was his in early childhood, as it was man's in the early preconscious childhood of the race. This is cotention. This is integration. This is man come to himself. (1949)[19]

To reformulate the technique specific to our procedure from the enlarged background of the soma's cotentive function, this technique requires, as far as my own subjective experience discloses, that one recognize his incessant preoccupation with mental images possessing an affect-coloring of greater or less intensity. This is the affect-element which, in attaching itself to the image or symbol, constitutes partitive attention or ditention. So that one's first recourse is to arrest such affect-images because of their functional disparity in relation to the organism as a whole. Through repeated experimentation my associates and I were at pains to verify that the tension about the eyes, while not the primary factor in ditention, constitutes an intrinsic part of the neuromuscular pattern involved.

Through daily experiment we found that these autopathic preoccupations invariably consist of obsessive fantasies having to do with one's "normal" satisfactions or denials—with one's liking or disliking, with his claims and frustrations, his rights and their infringement, his happiness or disappointment, and so on *ad infinitum*. These ruminations were seen to form the warp and woof of the loves and lusts of the "normal" as well as of the "neurotic," of his greeds and his grouches, his fears, his suspicions, his self-pity, pride, guilt, shame; his righteousness, his hardness and intolerance, his feeble dependence and his wayward sentimentalities. But again and again it was shown that, however unsuspected by the so-called normal wayfarer, such dichotomous preoccupations are in one form or another the confirmed habit of us all. They are the substance of ditention. They are the structure of the social neurosis. Whether waking or sleeping, we are granted no respite from these automatic preoccupations. Indeed, just as one is taken quite out of himself in his pursuit of the flight of a bird or hunted animal, so is one taken out of himself in his pursuit of these idle affects and fantasies.

So that we found ourselves trying to sense and adjust the imbalance of the eyes. As is one's recourse with any other group of muscles, the effort was to place attention upon the eyes and through the internal awareness or observation of them to relax and rest them. But, as I have indicated, observation of the functional area localized within the symbolic segment did not readily lead to permanent rest and reintegration of the muscle-contractions involved. So accustomed is this area to discrepant or disparate oculomotor tensions due to man's habitual interrelational affects, that an attempt to bring about a balance of these tensions was unwelcome and caused resistance or stress. It caused resistance or stress from which we tended automatically to seek comfort again in affect-projection or ditention, in automatically darting back to our accustomed images and their precious affect-attachments— to the various interrelational stimuli associated with the preservation of the social self-image.

But as more and more one recalls himself to himself, he is reminded that he is a student and that his field of research is the interrelational activation of man himself. Once more he sets to work. Again the eyes are closed. Again there is the darkness in front of him. Once more there is the central point and the black curtain before his brain. Again its fixated images and their affects are excluded. Again they are replaced by a sense of stress—of stress in the eyes and forehead. But, mind you, one is not *thinking*. One does not reach the phylobiological goal through mental information or knowledge. Not any more than one learns to dance through information or *knowing* about dancing. You dance or you don't dance according to your kinesthetic drill in the proper sequence of the dance steps. Similarly, one does not gain touch with the organism's neurosis through a mental acquaintance with it. One acquires an internal appreciation of tensions internal to the organism, and observations are based solely upon the internal sense or sensation of these tensions. And so, one's research is now not in the field of thought where all that he has known as research has hitherto lain. The research of the student of phylobiology is within the naked sensation or his own organism—the organism of man. Once more, then, the sense of stress is resumed, and despite the constantly recurring tendency to distraction and to the abandonment of experimentation in favor of tradition and habituation—of affect and self-image—the student holds on. He devotes himself disinterestedly to his material—to the objective material he senses within a segment of his own organism.

The task is unwelcome, and until this deeper phase of man's consciousness has become familiar, accustomed, he feels himself to be alone in it. Momentarily he *is* alone—alone in his feeling. Man does not like to feel that he is alone. It is not natural, not biological, to be alone—not as an individual or as a community cut off from other individuals or communities of our kind. But conscious of himself as a student of research in the field of his own—of man's—internally deviate tensions, the substance of the student's effort is precisely to recover contact with his kind, to recover the function of his organism in its total phylic feeling and integrity, and to renew continuity with other individuals, with all individuals, upon this common organismic basis. And so he works on.

With his increasing observation of the sensation caused by the partitive stress of the separate "I"-persona, there develops concurrently the sense of a larger background, of a background that is *not* affective, partitive, ditentive, that is *not* the "I"-persona, but that is the primary organism of man in its native spontaneous continuity and solidarity. With this phase of his experiment the student begins to sense the positive aspect of his inquiry. He begins to sense his own native organism with its uninhibited, non-affective interests. And thus is born the sensation of syntonicity—of *co*-tention or common tension.

With the sensing of this total organismic tone or balance of tensions and the corresponding absence of partitive images, one's preoccupations with idle fantasies based upon acquisitive security correspondingly fall away. Instead, the organism senses its relation to the environment and to others as an integral element within an integral organismic unit. Through this procedure the vast material of the organism's personal and social affects becomes increasingly set off from and contrasted with the more permanent matrix of the organism's motivation as a phylum. Where this technique has been persisted in by a group of people over a sufficient period of time, the barriers to common interests and activities artificially set up by the socially prevalent "I"-persona are let down in behalf of the common interests and activities that make for the survival of the individual and the group as a phylic whole.

This discussion of our phylophysiological technique set out with the description of the muscular tone or tension perceptible about the eyes. But we soon saw that these ocular tensions afforded but a clue—that they were only a fragment of the disordered pattern responsible for man's difficulty of adaptation or for his disbehavior. From this fragmentary beginning, however, a larger area of neurodynamic tension became increasingly susceptible of observation. We now became sensible of an entire brain pattern that more and more lent itself to demarcation and control. Abrogating customary "thinking" with its adherent affects, we intercepted the mechanism of projection and, instead, observed the mechanism that projects.

With this more encompassing sensation of stress or tension there was disclosed the phenomenon of ditention. But ditention is not the problem of any individual or of any group of individuals. It is the problem of man. The Lifwynn Laboratory* is but the nucleus of this larger program of social readjustment. There can be no true laboratory of behavior until there is the laboratory of man. Where it is a question of human conflict, it is the common tension of common men the world over to which we must look for the answer. (1949)[20]

---

* The setting for Burrow's research.-Ed.

Source Notes

[1] *The Structure of Insanity*, p. 75
[2] *The Neurosis of Man*, p. 69
[3] *The Biology of Human Conflict*, pp. 115–16
[4] *The Structure of Insanity*, pp. 67–68
[5] *The Neurosis of Man*, pp. 78–79
[6] "Prescription for Peace," pp. 103–06
[7] "The Social Neurosis," p. 37
[8] *The Biology of Human Conflict*, pp. 286–88
[9] *The Neurosis of Man*, pp. 238–40
[10] "Kymograph Records of Neuromuscular (Respiratory) Patterns in Relation to Behavior Disorders," p. 177
[11] *The Neurosis of Man*, pp. 241–42
[12] "Prescription for Peace," p. 110
[13] *The Biology of Human Conflict*, pp. 288–89
[14] *Ibid.*, p. 330
[15] *The Neurosis of Man*, pp. 243–44
[16] *Ibid.*, pp. 247–50
[17] *A Search for Man's Sanity*, pp. 360–62
[18] *Science and Man's Behavior*, pp. 95–96
[19] *The Neurosis of Man*, pp. 220–23
[20] *Ibid.*, pp. 253–58

V

Working with Tensions

Editor's Note

This chapter reports the results of instrumental studies documenting physiological changes that occurred when subjects shifted from ditention to cotention. From 1937 on, The Lifwynn Laboratory investigated respiration, eye-movements, brainwaves, and other aspects of physiological function in various experimental conditions. These studies showed clear differences between the two attentional modes and provided evidence that profound internal alterations, noted by the research group in cotention, were reflected in the physiological processes studied.

In addition, this chapter contains letters to students of Burrow's who had written him about their own practice of the cotentive technique. Burrow's replies—and other letters included in this chapter—show how he addressed the individual within his or her own setting and problems, without losing sight of the societal implications of phylobiological research.

In a letter to his associate, William Galt, Burrow describes his own practice with the internal shift from ditention to cotention. As indicated in the previous chapter (p. 89–90), he set aside periods during the day and night for such proprioceptive experimentation, that is, for perception of the subtle sensations in the area of the eyes associated with ditention. The attentional shift which took place in these practice sessions carried over into other daily activities, but he speaks in his letter to Galt of the difficulty of establishing cotention as an automatic habit (p. 126). "It is only as cotention becomes a community expression," he writes (p. 130), "that there will be an automatic modification of customary affective, or socially subversive, behavior."

These reservations, however, did not affect the instrumental experimentation. It required Burrow and other subjects to shift at a given signal from ditention to cotention and vice versa. It was found that this could be done readily and that the physiological changes being recorded took place at once.

There was very early with me the observation of alterations in the respiratory rhythm during attempts at cotention. This was at first a subjective and quite vague impression. But after many months it became evident that the rate of respiration was markedly slowed in the cotentive pattern of reaction.

The situation was similar with regard to changes occurring in the eyes. With the sense of tension in the region of the eyes coincident with the induction of cotention, I experienced a distinct sensation of ocular convergence, along with marked diminution in the number of blink reflexes. The alterations were slight and therefore not readily observable. Nevertheless it was possible to obtain substantial indication of modifications in the eyes coincident with cotention.

Following these early tentative observations, it became the experimental interest of my associates and myself to measure the physiological concomitants of the ditentive and cotentive behavior-patterns, and record any changes in the organism's physiology resulting from a shift from one to the other of these contrasting behavior-modes. I should emphasize, however, that this instrumental aspect of our studies is closely correlated with our earlier investigations in phyloanalysis. For it was only the many years spent in the frustration of social affects that ultimately led to our internal discrimination between the cotentive and the ditentive pattern of behavior. These years devoted to the analysis of the group as an integral biological unit afforded an indispensable background of experience and furnished the conditions that made possible the instrumental experiments.

These studies have centered chiefly on oculomotor behavior, respiratory reactions, and brain-wave patterning in the ditentive and in the cotentive mode of the organism's adaptation. Some investigations were also made of metabolism and of oxygen absorption and utilization in the two attentional patterns, and we conducted exploratory experiments on electrocardiographic responses.

A description of the detailed procedures that were followed in the various experiments, together with graphs and tables presenting the results, is included in the volume, *The Neurosis of Man*, as an appendix* and I shall here make brief mention of only the chief findings. These were (1) A marked and consistent slowing of the respiratory rate in cotention as compared with ditention, the decrease in rate in cotention being accompanied by an increase in the thoracic and abdominal amplitude of the respiratory movements.** (2) A reduction in number of eye-movements in cotention. This reduction during cotention occurs not only when the eyes are closed, or when they are directed straight ahead and no specific task or stimulation is imposed, but also under a wide variety of stimulus conditions. (3) A characteristic and consistent alteration in the brain-wave pattern during cotention. This altera-

---

* This appendix appears in both *The Neurosis of Man* and *Science and Man's Behavior*. (References are listed in the bibliography.)
See also:
   Burrow, Trigant, "Kymograph Records of Neuromuscular (Respiratory) Patterns in Relation to Behavior Disorders," 1941
   Burrow, Trigant and Galt, William, "Electroencephalographic Recordings of Varying Aspects of Attention in Relation to Behavior," 1945
   Burrow, Trigant and Syz, Hans, "Two Modes of Social Adaptation and Their Concomitants in Ocular Movements," 1949.-Ed.

** In addition, measurements of minute volume of air inspired, tidal air and oxygen utilization showed that "in cotention when a smaller volume of air is breathed per minute, a larger part of the available oxygen is utilized than under conditions of normal attention." See "Kymograph Records of Neuromuscular (Respiratory) Patterns in Relation to Behavior Disorders." pp. 181–182.-Ed.

tion consists of a reduction in alpha-time and a general diminution in cortical potential, which is most pronounced in the motor regions.

Respiration is, of course, a function of central importance in the maintenance of life. The part it plays in our everyday experience has long been familiar to us in such expressions as "the breath of life," "a sigh of relief," and in the converse implication of the phrase "choked with rage." A great deal of experimentation has been done on the physiological processes and the nervous mechanisms involved in breathing,* and on the relation of respiration to behavior and its disorders.** Respiratory irregularities and difficulties have been found to have a close association with emotional disturbances and with nervous and mental disorders.*** We are all familiar with the breathing irregu-

---

* Gesell, Robert, "Respiration and its Adjustments," *Annual Review of Physiology*, 1939, Vol. I, pp. 185–216.

  Hess, W. R., *Die Regulierungen des Blutkreislaufes und der Atmung*, Leipzig, Georg Thieme, 1931, pp. 137.

  ———, *Das Zwischenhirn und die Regulation von Kreislauf und Atmung*, Leipzig, Georg Thieme, 1938, pp. 137.

  Schmidt, Carl F., "The Respiration," in MacLeod's *Physiology in Modern Medicine*, St. Louis, The Mosby Co., 1941, pp. 534–710.

  Schmidt, Carl F., and Comroe, J. H., "Respiration," *Annual Review of Physiology*, 1941, Vol. 3, pp. 151–84.

** Finesinger, Jacob E., "Effect of Pleasant and Unpleasant Ideas on Respiration in Psychoneurotic Patients," *Archives of Neurology and Psychiatry*, 1939, Vol. 42, pp. 425–90.

  Lehmann, Alfr., *Grundzüge der Psychophysiologie*, Leipzig, O. R. Reisland, 1912, pp. x, 742.

  Winkler, C., "Attention and Respiration," *Proceedings of the Royal Academy of Sciences*, Amsterdam, 1899, Vol. 1, pp. 121–38.

  Wyss, W. H. von, "Einfluss psychischer Vorgänge auf Atmung, Pulsfrequenz, Blutdruck und Blutverteilung," *Handbuch der normalen und pathologischen Physiologie*, Berlin, Springer, 1931, Vol. 16, pp. 1261–88.

  Zoneff, P., and Meumann, E., "Ueber Begleiterscheinungen psychischer Vorgänge in Athem und Puls," *Philosophische Studien*, 1903, Vol. 18, pp. 1–113.

*** It is noteworthy in this connection that somatic conditions such as pulmonary tuberculosis and asthma have not infrequently been found to be as-

larities produced by an intense emotional response. But a review of the experimental data assembled by various investigators regarding modifications of breathing in attention, in mental effort, in emotional situations and in other psychological or behavioristic action-patterns did not reveal respiratory changes of the type we have found to be consistently present in cotention.

As regards eye-movements, we know that they are intimately connected with the employment of the symbolic mechanism as well as with the organism's total adaptation to the environment. They play an important role in thinking and imagination.* The eyes are constantly in motion when one is engaged in projective or perceptual processes. So that one might well expect a difference in the motor behavior of the eyes during ditention as compared with cotention, that is, in the restless, competitive mood of "normal" thinking and feeling as compared with the more collected, integrated mood of the organism's total bionomic orienta-

---

sociated with personality conflicts and that these conflicts may be important factors in the onset and course of these diseases.

Brown, Lawrason, "The Mental Aspect in the Etiology and Treatment of Pulmonary Tuberculosis," *International Clinics,* 1933, Vol. III, 43rd Series, pp. 149–74.

French, Thomas N., and Alexander, Franz, "Psychogenic Factors in Bronchial Asthma, Part I," *Psychosomatic Medicine Monograph IV,* 1941, pp. 236.

Hartz, Jerome, "Tuberculosis and Personality Conflicts," *Psychosomatic Medicine,* 1944, Vol. VI, pp. 17–22.

Leavitt, Harry C., "Bronchial Asthma in Functional Psychoses," *Psychosomatic Medicine,* 1943, Vol. V, pp. 39–41.

Rubin, Sidney, and Moses, Leon, "Electroencephalographic Studies in Asthma with some Personality Correlates," *Psychosomatic Medicine,* 1944, Vol. VI, pp. 31–9.

Shultz, Irvin T., "The Emotions of the Tubercular: A Review and an Analysis," *The Journal of Abnormal and Social Psychology,* 1942, Vol. 37, pp. 260–3.

* Jacobson, Edmund, "Electrophysiology of Mental Activities," *American Journal of Psychology,* 1932, Vol. XLIV, pp. 677–94.

tion. It is quite understandable, indeed, that both respiration and eye-movements should constitute indicators of differing behavior-constellations and that the tensional pattern of ditention as of cotention should be reflected in modifications in these physiological systems.

From previous investigations of brain-wave patterns we know that modifications in the physiological function of the brain are reflected in changes in cortical potential. These changes are most marked in brain lesions and in convulsive disorders.[*] But behavior-disorders of a functional type also show a large percentage of altered electrical pictures.[**] And even such temporary functional states as sleep and sleepiness cause variations in brain-wave patterns.[***] It is there-

---

[*] Case, Theodore J., and Bucy, Paul C., "Localization of Cerebral Lesions by Electroencephalography," *Journal of Neurophysiology*, 1938, Vol. I, pp. 245–61.

Gibbs, Frederic A., Davis, Hallowell, and Lennox, William G., "The Electroencephalogram in Epilepsy and in Conditions of Impaired Consciousness," *Archives of Neurology and Psychiatry*, 1935, Vol. 34, pp. 1133–48.

Gibbs, Frederic A., Lennox, William G., and Gibbs, Erna L., "The Electroencephalogram in Diagnosis and in Localization of Epileptic Seizures," *Archives of Neurology and Psychiatry*, 1936, Vol. 36, pp. 1225–35.

Walter, W. Grey, "The Electroencephalogram in Cases of Cerebral Tumour," *Proceedings of the Royal Society of Medicine*, 1937, Vol. 30, pp. 579–98.

Gibbs, Frederic A., and Gibbs, Erna L., *Atlas of Electroencephalography*, 1941, Cambridge, Massachusetts, pp. 221.

[**] Davis, Pauline A., and Davis, Hallowell, "The Electroencephalograms of Psychotic Patients," *The American Journal of Psychiatry*, 1939, Vol. 95, pp. 1007–25.

Jasper, Herbert H., Solomon, Philip, and Bradley, Charles, "Electroencephalographic Analyses of Behavior Problem Children," *The American Journal of Psychiatry*, 1938, Vol. 95, pp. 641–58.

Travis, Lee Edward, and Malamud, William, "Brain Potentials from Normal Subjects, Stutterers and Schizophrenic Patients," *The American Journal of Psychiatry*, 1937, Vol. 93, pp. 929–36.

[***] Loomis, Alfred L., Harvey, E. Newton, and Hobart, Garret A., III, "Potential Rhythms of the Cerebral Cortex during Sleep," *Science*, 1935, Vol. 81, pp. 597–98;

fore not surprising that we should find measurable differences in the electrical activity of the brain in the
contrasting types of adaptation represented by cotention and ditention, or that these differences should be
reflected in characteristic patterns of cerebral potential. Undoubtedly Berger's prediction of the wide
applicability of electroencephalography to social as
well as to clinical behavior-disorders will be more and
more verified as further studies serve to establish the
place of this significant tool in the understanding and
betterment of human relations.* (1949)[1]

With regard to the instructions given to student
subjects in our respiratory experiments, it has been my
procedure to have the subject assume a recumbent
posture or a comfortable sitting position. I then in-
struct him to close his eyes and, as far as possible,
maintain them in a state of relaxation. I explain that
this procedure is assisted by letting the eyes rest upon
a point which he may picture as forming the center
of the curtain of darkness in front of him. By way of
helping the student to attain his visual fixation solely
through his kinesthetic sense of the eyes, I usually cite
the difference between holding the outstretched arm
steady by grasping a stationary object, and holding the
arm steady without the aid of this external support. In
the latter case the subject's sole guide as to its position
is his sensation of the weight and muscular tension in
the outstretched arm. In order to avoid introducing an
element of suggestion, our instructions to subjects
were restricted to the simple formula just outlined.

"Distribution of Disturbance-Patterns in the Human Electroencephalogram, with Special Reference to Sleep," *Journal of Neurophysiology*, 1938,
Vol. I, pp. 413–30.

* Gibbs, Frederick A., and Gibbs, Erna L., Dedication in *Atlas of Electroencephalography*, 1941, Cambridge, Massachusetts, pp. 221.

The fact cannot be too strongly stressed, however, that by virtue of neuromuscular reaction-habits long established within the species, man is now averse to any alteration which challenges his accustomed neuromuscular pattern of adaptation. On this account it should be emphasized that it was necessary to repeat the instructions very many times.

It may be added that the respiratory alterations set in immediately with the alteration of the attentional pattern. They occurred automatically and were not brought about by any voluntary effort or conscious manipulation. The respiratory changes, as they occur during cotention, do not show any similarity to the slight modifications observed under conditions in which the subject focuses upon external objects or upon bodily tensions in regions other than those of the symbolic segment. In the period of normal attention immediately following cotention there was no compensatory acceleration in the breathing rate. But where subjects were instructed to retard the frequency of breathing consciously, while maintaining normal attention, the records showed a subsequent acceleration. (1941)[2]

Needless to say, increased experience in cotention may add further indication of physiological changes, or may materially modify the indications already obtained.* There are other physiological areas of re-

---

* From *Science and Man's Behavior*, p. 98, quoting a letter to Dr. David Katz, April 1949:

In those of us in whom cotention has become a quite customary procedure there is already an indication of modification in recent experiments. There is not now the very marked retardation in the breathing-rhythm, with the shift to the cotentive pattern. Apparently the extremely slow breathing-curves we obtained in the early period of our investigations of cotention are to be understood in part as a function of that initial stage in the experimentation. Certainly, as cotention became more habitual—as it be-

sponse that could be studied, and it is obvious that the present findings should be checked on a larger series of subjects. It should be remembered, however, that a prerequisite for the subject in such experiments is his acquirement of the consistent ability to abrogate affective projections and regain the organism's central, cotentive pattern. As already noted, this has not proved an easy task—at least for the pioneer students in this field—so that at first only a small number of subjects were available for instrumental experimentation. Keeping these restrictions in mind, we may say that the instrumental studies of The Lifwynn Laboratory have demonstrated the concomitance of marked and consistent physiological alterations with the induction of the pattern of cotention.

It should be clearly understood that, valuable and significant as our instrumental recordings may be, they are in a sense quite incidental to our major thesis. No student, of course, should expect to find the millennium in instrumental records, but he must be especially warned against the seductive blandishments of graphs that undertake to chart human behavior. Although these tracings show a difference in the organism's internal reaction according as the organism responds directly or indirectly to its environment, they offer only an external indication of this difference. Undoubtedly, individuals and social communities are in need of a basic alteration in behavior-adaptation, but they will find this needed alteration only through specific physiological adjustments internal to themselves.

---

came more a matter of routine among us—the characteristic respiratory rate increased. It still differs, however, from the rate prevailing in ditention. I am just now in the process of getting together some experimental data on this matter and hope to publish it in the near future. (Burrow did not live to complete this experimentation.—Ed.)

And so, while giving full due to instrumental recordings of alterations in this or that physiological system, I feel it important to emphasize once more that our starting-point and our ending-point is the internal perception of the organism's pattern of behavior as a whole. And by organism as a whole I mean the phylobiological organism of man. Graphs of physiological changes may possess value for us only as they offer corroboration of internal phylic modifications registered by us through the internally controlled technique of phyloanalysis. (1949)[3]

Cotention originated as a group process and is, therefore, essentially a social as well as an individual phenomenon. This is of interest in connection with our observation that the individual is assisted in recovering his organism's cotentive pattern to the degree in which he finds himself one of a group whose purpose is, in general, hospitable to this altered mode of adaptation.* The organismic correspondence between the cotentive pattern existing in the individual and this same pattern as it exists in the group is of vital import from the point of view of human behavior. To be able to trace the biological parallel between the ontogenetic and the phylogenetic aspects of man's behavior, even in the midst of the widespread chaos existing in the world today, possesses deep sociobiological significance. This reversion to organismic type should, when given practical social application, contribute

---

* From *Science and Man's Behavior*, p. 99, quoting the letter to Dr. David Katz, April 1949: Whether this adjustment can be obtained without some background of discipline in group-analysis is not a question which I am at the moment prepared to answer categorically. Certainly, the long and intensive schedule followed by our original research group will not need to be repeated by other groups in order to achieve the cotentive pattern of behavioral adaptation.

materially to preserve the primary viability of man's organism in both its individual and its community processes. (1941)[4]

It may be that some day we shall discover certain drugs or some combination of drugs which, in influencing special brain-areas, will facilitate the induction and maintenance of the pattern of cotention. Certainly there is ground for the expectation that with improved instrumental methods it will be possible to discover technical facilities that will assist students to discriminate between the partitive and the total pattern of reaction. As I have repeatedly emphasized, though, this needed behavioral readjustment involves a behavior-pattern that belongs to man as a race or species. Such a behavior-pattern, therefore, can only be reinstated by man as an integral group or community. In the meantime there is here at least the beginning of an attempt to meet a functional anomaly in man's development with a functional technique of adaptation such as should reestablish man's organismic balance in the field of his sociobiological interrelations. (1949)[5]

*I think, if I were you, I would not be too confident that Krishnamurti and I are of the same trend. He has the words perhaps, but not the music. Or, if you like (most people *would* like, no doubt) he has the music and not the words. My point is only that he hasn't both—he hasn't coordinated the organism's intero-with its extero-ceptive function. I heard Krishnamurti lecture. I read a book of his. He is fascinating. He is exquisitely facile mentally. I love all that sort of thing but, like so many things I love, participation in it is sheer voluptuous indulgence with me. It lacks the

---

* From a letter to Jessie Sampter.

robustness of actuality, of direct contact with the raw
materials of reality. But here are words again and not
music or, as I said before, vice versa. It isn't the total
organism functioning in coordination with its kind in
their common relation to the environment. That's a
physiological problem. That it is internal makes it not
less but more physiological. It is physiology not
looked at or worded over, so to speak. We are—all of
us—such picture people and all our pictorial produc-
tions resting upon the wide and limitless canvas of "I."
Something must be done. Something will be done.
Something is, I devoutly believe, at this moment *being
done*. It is this process which in a way we of The Lifwynn Foundation seem trying to articulate—not in
words or music or in any external combination of the
two, but through their intrinsic coordination in actual
communal (not communistic—that's the image again—
but physiological) living. Your head and my head
won't reach our goal, no more will your heart or mine,
however ardent our attack. The problem is biological,
and it is internal, and I know of nothing so baffling.
(1937)[6]

    *People do not at all credit the physiology of their
social tensions, the tensions coincident with group interchange. We know very well the physiological tensions that accompany individual states of health, as of
ill health. We know, for example, the physiological
stress or tension of an individual's revulsion as expressed in the reaction of nausea. But the contrast in
physiological tension that accompanies man's healthy
and his unhealthy social interrelations we do not
realize. We do not sense the internal difference between one's falsely separate sense of identity and our

---

* From a letter to Herbert Read.

sense as a common race or species of our common
identity. I do not think we shall heal the pain of our
differences except as we learn to define within ourselves the presence of these contrasting patterns.
(1948)[7]

The result of our experiment has been a basic alteration among us toward the organism's primary reac-
tion-trend and a fundamental revaluation in personal
and social outlooks. I do not mean that as a group we
have been "successful," that having been distrait,
maladjusted elements in a maladjusted ("normal")
community, we were at last made whole, and that finding ourselves duly shriven we were now prepared to
bring others into the light. God forbid! As well a smug
and neatly adjusted individual as a smug and neatly
adjusted community or "group." If I understand the
meaning of group—if I understand the biological import of group in the sense of an organismic unit integrated of elements that are structurally and functionally homogeneous, the only group of real significance
in human behavior is the behavior-whole represented
in the organism of man as a phylum. The members of
our own group-organization seemed, like other normal
individuals, under the thrall of what I might call a
widespread social "apraxia"—a social apraxia or a
community inadvertence in function adventitiously
induced in man's behavior. Our endeavors aimed,
therefore, toward the achievement of a creative synthesis of our processes as they may become internally
appreciable within the wider unit composing the organism of man as a species. (1937)[8]

*I too have felt that cotention was very much in the

---

* From a letter to Alfreda Galt.

background with you and with William. But I don't see
how it could have been otherwise. The pattern—the
internal pattern of our adaptation—is not personal, not
individual. It is social, and no individual can possibly
control it. It would be like expecting a muscle of the
forearm to govern the tone or tensional pattern of the
body's muscular system as a whole. It is of course the
other way round. It is the total pattern that governs the
behavior of the individual element or part. One does
have, it seems to me, the opportunity, or one can make
the opportunity when one is alone—between switch-
ing out one's light at night and the moment of the day's
return in the morning—to sense one's partitive confusion and to insist on maintaining the sense of one's
perturbed and agitated state, however impotent one
may be to do anything about it *beyond the mere sensing of it*. But damn it, we don't do that. We keep right
on too often in our abject, externally dictated or socially conditioned whirl. It is instinctive that with distress there is the organism's attention to the distressed
part or organ. The very animals seek protection and
quiet and a period of rehabilitation. But with this dislocation in man's adaptation to realities he is too distorted, his attention is too led away by the false interests of suggestion and habit and social tradition for him
to know, to have any realizing sense of his distorted
condition as an organism.

That is the problem. That is the task—somehow
holding still against the agitations of our external, superficial and purely fanciful excitements. As far as my
own experience goes, this exercise in self-collected-
ness, however incomplete, however ineffectual—this
passive restoration of total sensation and the physical
awareness of the stress and conflict that one's agitation

imposes physiologically—does seem essential toward inculcating an appreciation of our opportunity as a laboratory of consensual observers. This does seem to me a very significant part of our research task. But we always have to have "results," immediate results. I mean that mentally we are spoiled and impatient. We are not willing to bring the same research patience to the observation of our own wheeling, gyrating tendencies of feeling and thinking that we demand of ourselves in any other field of objective investigation.

Of course our efforts are defeated again and again. But what does one expect of research? Why must we look for child's play where there is question of an extremely serious problem in subjectively deflected reactions? But no, the baby has got to be entertained. Tootsy Wootsy has always been taken up and bounced when his or her little moments of impatience have vented themselves in whimpering and complaint. But can we not as adults take our childishness in hand, not with the usual recourses or from the usual mental or moralistic background, but as a disturbance in the organism's balance, in the organismic balance subjectively of myself or yourself or whoever's self? How stupid we are not to grapple with our problem, but to be always disheartened by repeated defeat. (1945)[9]

*I would say "yes," that you're "on the right track." But I'd feel the need to qualify this statement or at least to amplify it. "You" (as we've said before surely) might be on the right track and your organism very far off of it. You'll be saying: "Now he's getting rough again." But surely we have learned to discriminate between *me* and *man*, between what I like or aspire to in

---

* From a letter to a student.

my purely partitive (affecto-symbolic) identity and what is fitting to me as a totally integrated organism. There is so much one could say and so many ways of saying it. I hardly know where to begin.

I think you've done good work. I think you are doing good work. You are intelligent and you are earnest. The rest will come of itself with consistent adherence to a very simple, if baffling, technique. You need not bother. We need not be concerned. Our concern is for "me." "Me" has thrust itself into the foreground and interrupted the consistent pursuit of our technique—the technique of cotention. You expressed it well in your letter. "Yours," you said in effect, "is not to reason why, yours is but to do—to cotend." Have you forgotten? How often we all forget! Do not let it trouble you. All of us apparently still insist upon believing that cotention, or integration, is some sort of stunt, rather than a fixed habit of total phyloorganismic balance. Slowly the organism seems to be inculcating in us what all our philosophies do not yet even begin to suspect.

In feeling that "mental understanding" of our endeavor is not the answer, your thought comes close to touching bottom. I wager you would under no circumstances have expressed yourself in these terms but for some actual experience with cotention. One cannot *think* clearly or inclusively apart from his ability to *feel* clearly and inclusively. It's amazing when one considers the extent to which we habitually credit this superficial trick of thought without reckoning upon the basis from which all thought arises—the organism's primary feeling or motivation!

I think we do not sufficiently sense the phylic implications of our thesis. We tend to think of me and

mine. We argue from the artificial premise of the symbolic "I"-persona, rather than from a basis that is organismically common and unitary throughout the race.
This is what words cannot say, will never say. This is
not a mental theory, but a physiological function.
Hence cotention, or the physiological adjustment that
stresses more and more the prior significance of the
phylic organism as a whole—a phylic principle that is
no less the individual's than it is the species'—in contrast to the merely socio-symbolic pattern that too commonly serves the private interest of the "I"-persona.

Your cowardice? It just doesn't exist. *Man* is the
coward. You (or I) are merely a symbol—a part-expression of man, the phylum. Being affectively bound up
with the symbol that you yourself have come to embody, you falsely identify yourself—your organism—
with this symbol of man—this mere affecto-symbolic
"I"-persona. But again "you" cannot realize this organismically in the absence of the organismic pattern
I've called "cotention." You see, all roads lead to this
central, primary pattern of behavior. But you have said
the same thing—that you cannot reach a (symbolic)
"cowardice" mentally, but only cotentively. I'm sure
that only the accidental circumstance that led to the
opportunity of group analysis and group living, with
its relentless frustration of habitually comforting social
affects, could ever have recovered, have unearthed the
phylic elements of man's feeling we are coming to
sense practically in cotention. But why do I say all
this? It is a familiar theme to you by now. I like to re-
fresh my memory, though, regarding data that have
meant much to me and that may some day become
deeply significant to man. (1943)[10]

*It seems too bad and yet, I know, so inevitable that you should be cudgeling your poor brains over a convulsive outbreak that you believe is your own when, in point of fact, it is but a small part of a world paroxysm. Whether overt or covert, whether in you or me, in the Axis powers or the democracies, the disorder is the same. As long as each of us thinks he is the universe, he will go on cudgeling what he believes to be his universal brains. Our job is to recognize the illness of man, and our own involvement as but a very tiny element in the larger disturbance of the race of man. Neither you nor I is as important as each of us believes himself to be. But we like our importance so we cling to our belief. (1943)[11]

**About your own plans toward a solution of your very pressing and oppressing problems of social adjustment and to your question as to "what I think of it all." You were speaking, you remember, chiefly of your plan, and that of your associates, to establish a remote colony somewhere and so "extricate yourselves from the deathly debris of this crumbling civilization." I do not at all see how you can withdraw this way from the sick muddle of things and not take me with you— me and the other millions of people that make up the common run of us. Unless you feel that our pain and confusion are less than yours or that we are less sensitive to it than you are, but I do not believe for a moment that this is your attitude. I could not imagine you, of all people, differentiating yourself from others in any such fashion. And yet your program of isolation for

---

* From a letter to another student.

** From a letter to James P. Cooney.

yourself and your group has definitely in it this element of discrimination, of setting yourselves apart.
Colonization seems a form of escape—a sort of running
away. I'd rather stand and take it. It seems healthier.
And what is more I think you would. I think you'd
rather stand with the rest of us, for all our stupidity and
inadequacies of feeling and motivation, than move
apart from us. And so, since you ask me, I'd weigh
carefully this idea of a colony of place and opportunity
and security. I'd think rather of the possibilities of a
colony of *thought* and *feeling* within the very midst of
the confused social community in which you and I find
ourselves. I think you might find restriction and cur-
tailment in any other course. I think you might find
your genuinely deep, human sympathies denied their
full expression in any setting other than the immediate
need and confusion of our common humanity. (1939)[12]

 *Last night before going to sleep I took serious
counsel with myself regarding the problem of my
(man's) incorrect behavior interrelationally. (I know
nothing of course about a subjective defect of adaptation in man, except as I know it in myself or subjectively.) I was going over the rationale of the situation—
the mechanism of man's tensional deflection (ditention) as it occurs in the symbolic segment. It seemed so
baffling, so elusive.

 I thought how long and, I think I may say, ear-
nestly I have been working on it without yet establishing cotention as a spontaneous habit—without correct-
ing the reflex habit of reaction as one corrects a verbal
error or a faulty muscular coordination. The problem
seemed very large and, as I say, baffling. So that I

---

* From a letter to William E. Galt.

found myself quite caught up—not altogether without
value, I think—in the mental or theoretical aspect of
the condition. Then, but very reluctantly, I began to
pull myself away from the fascination of my mere mental preoccupation with it. With difficulty and much resistance I began to remind myself of the feeling (empathic) nature of my (man's) problem, and so little by
little to let myself into, yield myself to the tensional or
stereognostic (and therefore internal, *non*-mental)
character of my (the organism's) task. The mental path
was barred, if the organism's basic need was to take its
course, and only the path of feeling remained to me.
And so the mental problem fell away, and with it the
affect and fret concomitant to it. Where the mental
stress or pain had been—in the frontal, orbital areas—
there was now a physiological, tensional stress that
stood out in its place (as "sensum") against a feel of the
organism as a non-mental, non-personal or phylic
whole. The problem was the recognition of the artificial demarcation between organism and symbolic segment and the gradual reabsorption of the digressive
element into the total somatic, the total tensional system.

   All this I write now, I know is purely mental,
purely conceptual. I know that when I return to bed to-
night, I may not go on in this vein, whatever its
theoretical value. I know that no laboratory procedure
occupies itself with concept, that its quarry is the recording of objective data, and that one may not escape
this canon of the laboratory when the laboratory happens to be one's own organic processes. (1943)[13]

   *Of course I am never going to help man in the fun-

---

* From a letter to Dr. Adolf Meyer.

damental reconstruction of his own behavior. Nobody is. It is only my long-conditioned habits of abstraction and isolation that ever led me to suppose I could. Man must avail himself of the discoveries of science to help himself. I do not doubt, though, that even now man is in his own way assisting himself, that he is somehow getting back to biological base, that all this world revolution—as ghastly, as insane, as destructive as it is—is somehow an expression of man's need to come to himself. My part, your part—the part of the social biologist, as I see it—is to use whatever authority we possess to assist this process of man's re-adaptation. It is to show as far as we can that man himself (and we along with him) is the only authority in matters of his own behavior, that this authority is internal to him, as it is internal to us, and that wherever we presume to *know*, wherever we presume to make an abstraction of this thing that is man's internal motivation (I am writing you just as the thoughts come to me) we are only deceiving ourselves and man. We are only adding to the obstruction, and retarding man's ultimate self-actualization. (1941)[14]

*Cotention is *nothing*. That is its difficulty. To people, to a race of people who are at all times, from birth to death, hot after *something*—everything—cotention seems, of course, unattainable.

We have a colossal job. People with a colossal job ordinarily apply their energies accordingly. But people who are hot after *something*—something mental—take a *laissez faire* attitude toward their job. They play about—giggling, coquetting or grieving, according to the direction in which this mental emotive

---

* From a letter to Alfreda Galt.

something—this visible addition to me, seems to lie.

Cotention is not the rub. It is ditention—the imaginary mental something man is vainly projecting at every moment. (1950)[15]

The technique of cotention, like any other technique, is acquired only through research, or "practice." No student will step lightly from ditention into cotention. Cotention is not a matter of intellectual acumen, but of intestinal fortitude. Its attainment demands constant repetition. The distractions are many and persistent, and the student must return again and again to his experimental task. I can give him no other formula than that of refusing to entertain his customary ideas or affect images, and thus gradually coming to perceive the segment that habitually projects the image.

With increasing practice the student will perceive this segment through the characteristic sense of local tension he experiences with the abrogation of his habitual ditentive interests. But this is research. It is research on the part of man's whole organism in respect to a deviate part-function of that same organism. The student is thus approaching for the first time a new field of experiment. Throughout his approach there will be a constant tendency in his own habitual and immediate behavior to discredit his task and to harken instead to the more welcome invitations of affect and ditention.

I do not know how it may seem to others, but I believe no one will strive to arrest an habitual reflex if the reflex offers no difficulty—no pain or impediment. If a habit presents no menace to the health of the organism, why should one wish to arrest it? As I have said, with my co-workers and myself there was much

pain and embarrassment in the emotional impact
brought about by the interrelational challenge and arrest of our habitual affects. And it was only under the
duress of this repeated trauma that a sense of the affront to the underlying physiological structures within
the forepart of the head was brought to awareness, and
finally caused the attention to shift from the affecto-
symbolic object (projection) to the physiological reaction underlying it.

I think that cotention will not attain practical realization as a phylic discipline except in the measure in
which communities of people are educated to the false
affect values, the surface (wishful) thinking, that now
determine their interrelational behavior in all its aspects—political, religious, economic, academic, industrial. Therefore one may not speak of the cotention
of the individual without of necessity presupposing
the restoration of the cotentive pattern of adaptation in
humanity at large—no more than he could speak of
eliminating tuberculosis in the individual and not in
the phylum. It is only as cotention becomes a community expression that there will be an automatic modification of customary affective, or socially subversive,
behavior. I cannot emphasize strongly enough our
position that neurosis is a social aberration, and that
the essential contribution of phylobiology to the
sphere of behavior research is its recognition of the
subjective constellation of reactions embodied in the
social "I"-persona—the field of man's partitive self in
action. This, and this alone, is cotention; this is the
meaning, the essence, of phylobiology. (1950)[16]

Source Notes

1 *The Neurosis of Man,* pp. 260–65
2 "Kymograph Records of Neuromuscular (Respiratory) Patterns in Relation to Behavior Disorders," pp. 177–80
3 *The Neurosis of Man,* pp. 265–68
4 "Kymograph Records of Neuromuscular (Respiratory) Patterns in Relation to Behavior Disorders," p. 183
5 *The Neurosis of Man,* pp. 266–67
6 *A Search for Man's Sanity,* pp. 341–42
7 *Science and Man's Behavior,* pp. 91–92
8 *The Biology of Human Conflict,* p. xl
9 *A Search for Man's Sanity,* pp. 480–81
10 *Ibid.,* pp. 454–56
11 *Ibid.,* p. 450
12 *Ibid.,* pp. 386–87
13 *Ibid.,* pp. 459–60
14 *Ibid.,* p. 427
15 *Ibid.,* p. 590
16 "Prescription for Peace," pp. 110–11

VI

The Global Whole

Editor's Note

What Burrow calls the "physiological self" is immediately accessible to each of us in the proprioceptive sensations and tensions we experience from moment to moment. However, the internal tensions he
identified as associated with defective interrelational
function are usually masked and overlaid by preoccupation with emotionally toned projections. Yet this
distorted tensional pattern can nevertheless be sensed
(with the help of the appropriate technique) against
the background of organismic feeling or cotention,
the common tension of the species. In doing so, Burrow tells us in the first selection in this chapter, contact is made with the energies of the phylic whole.
This chapter indeed deals with the phyloorganism in
its broadest aspect.

The final pages suggest how Burrow envisioned
the future of phylobiological research. Faced with
threats to the very survival of the race, the scientific
community must accept responsibility for instituting
a dispassionate investigation of the aberration it
shares with society at large. But the development of
such research cannot be left to any one group or
stratum. "A science of human behavior," Burrow
writes (p. 135), "is truly a science for the millions."

From the background of the preceding chapters we are now in a position to consider man, the organism, in a new and greatly expanded concept. We are in a position to keep dynamically alive the biological identity of individual and phylum, the inseparable continuity between the organism of man as ontosoma or individual, and as phylosoma or species. Man has falsely separated ontosoma from phylosoma, and this has caused modification in a pattern of tension that is internal to the organism. If the vast millions of individuals that constitute the race or phylosoma of man are to be restored to their intrinsic organismic matrix, it is necessary that man take conscious hold of this abnormal distortion of tension; that he recognize within himself the morbid process his artificial division entails. Contrary to popular assumption, man is not a symbolic abstraction; man—man, the phylum— is one's own ontosomatic self. (1949)[1]

Our insistence upon the necessity of keeping within us, as well as before us, the broad biological concept of man as a unitary, organismic phylum is by no means arbitrary. It is essential to the meaning of the present thesis that this inclusive definition of man as a unitary organism be sustained throughout the field of phylobiology and that we preserve in our own subjective outlook the altered frame of reference coincident with this more encompassing conception of the species as an organismic whole. (1949)[2]

The problem of phylobiology is the problem of the "I"-persona—the problem of man's self. This self of man is the self of everyone. It is the self of every "you" and of every "me." For the neurosis of man is world-wide; and a science of human behavior is truly a science for the millions. Just as medicine applies the remedy to the individual organism in which the disease occurs, so in the field of human behavior, if the disease resides within the organism of social man, the remedy must be applied to the social organism.

I hope I have made clear that as our inquiry is universal, as it deals with the subjective material of the distorted self—with *my* prejudices, *your* prejudices, and *the prejudices of us all*—our approach to this material can only be universal in scope. But in this inclusive approach it is required that the student of human behavior become an internal experimentalist; that he attain an altered frame of reference with respect to the internal feeling or mood of man. (1949)[3]

It is quite unthinkable that there should not exist for the phylosoma as a whole a definite functional norm, a determinable central constant that is as basic and dependable as the universal structural norm recognized as protoplasm. It is unthinkable that there should not exist a primary principle of functional constancy or interrelational balance within the phyloorganism that discloses deviations in function correlative to those existing in the structural sphere. The presence of such a primary balance of function is inherent in the principle of phyloorganismic homeostasis. Deviations from this consistency of function are to be seen in the various expressions of mental disorders, individual and social—in phobias, hysterical paralyses, unwarranted suspicions, states of elation and depression, disorders within the sexual sphere, etc., as well as in crime, industrial conflict, political dissension and war.

Phylobiology, therefore, requires that we recognize within the phyloorganism a principle of behavioral function that is primary and that corresponds to the primary structural principle of protoplasm. (1949)[4]

There is required an approach that is consistent with an *applied anthropology*. Man's study of man must deal with the vital phenomenon of the organism's action and reaction precisely as it deals with this phenomenon in all other living forms. In short, there is demanded an anthropology that is not purely traditional or historic, but an anthropology that offers the student direct functional impact with the daily reactions of himself and his fellows—an anthropology that is medical as well as social and in which material and observation have to do with behavioral processes of immediate and dynamic insistency. It will have to do with subjective sensations and reactions as they arise out of the generic solidarity of man as a species. (1949)[5]

There is need of a science that is not involved *a priori* in the prevailing premise of normality with its partisan self-assertion and its corresponding self-defense. We are in need of a science that clearly disavows the two-way policy of behavior whereby any individual, group or nation is arbitrarily "right" as over against the individual, group or nation which on this same divisive premise is proscribed as "wrong." For we must recognize that the habitual attitude of "rightness" underlying all interrelational conflict betrays an equally wishful, arbitrary state of mind in each of the contending parties.* There is required an objective science that examines dispassionately into the nature

---

* It must also be recognized, of course, that where there exists agreement between individuals or groups on the ground of mutual rights that are arbitrary, the situation is no more stable or dependable than where there exists dissension between them on grounds of these same arbitrary rights.

of this esoteric "rightness" now regarded subjectively as the private prerogative of each opposed faction. (1949)[6]

When people come to realize that the disease is universal, they will begin to recognize for the first time what is their real, their inherent need. This need is the stabilization of their own processes, of their individual and social processes. It is the need to see that disorder resides within the tissues of phylic man, and that only an immediate phylic approach to the *present*—to man's immediate global insecurity—can disclose the cause of his conflict and confusion.

Man may delude himself only with respect to past and future. His integrity, his security, the dependability of his relationship to the environment are inevitably bound up with his relationship to the present and to himself. When man will be brought to a sense of the plight in which he finds himself today; when, refusing to indulge in either memories or hopes, he is brought up short with the stark immediacy of the moment, man will at last take hold of his own processes in relation to the environment.

Man stands in need of a phyloanalysis—an analysis of his own organism, an analysis of the phyloorganism of the species. This effort to meet the present, to see what is to be done in regard to man's own behavior, his own feeling, and to do it now, has been the central endeavor of my co-workers and myself of The Lifwynn Laboratory. (1949)[7]

It is in keeping with the disordered development of internal man that atomic energy should first have been used as a destructive agent. Obviously man's disordered behavior is in the moment more powerful than his clear thinking, feeling and doing—than his own basic adaptation in respect to the external surroundings. This circumstance is a commentary upon man as a species. But in the disturbed state of man's feeling-life it could not be otherwise. The fact remains that atomic energy was first employed as a means of destruction, and by nations that presumably represent an enlightened form of government. This circumstance, however, is relatively negligible beside the appalling fact that science itself should have approved of its use as a means of destroying human life. It is indeed significant that in its largest opportunity even the creative inventiveness of science should have succumbed to the domination of the generic disorder in adaptation that marks the behavior of the species. (1949)[8]

Is it possible for man to realize that the weapon of offense we call the atomic bomb has really arisen within his own organism? Is it possible for him to realize that the correction of this destructive agent can also arise only within his own organism? But if we are to attain a realizing sense that the cause of man's hostility to man lies within ourselves, it is necessary that we somehow recast completely our subjective habits of feeling and thinking—that we recoil with cold, objective analysis upon our own cherished prepossessions. The harmful agent is not uranium and the splitting of its atom. It is the mind of man and its split mood; it is man's schizophrenic bent towards world inequality and dissension. (1949)[9]

Our problem, then, is not one that calls so much for a needed adjustment in our habitual way of thinking as it calls for a fundamentally reorganized instrument with which to think. For this deficiency in appraising man's own behavior is internal and intrinsic to the organism of man himself. The defect is one that constitutes an impediment within our own subjective machinery as it relates itself to others and to the world shared in common by us. And so the needed adjustment demands our biological recognition and application of a totally altered method of investigation. (1937)[10]

On the basis of the researches of my associates and myself, the total organism of man became a new instrument of observation in the field of human behavior. These researches made evident that there is no valid objective observation in the field of interrelational behavior except as the observer senses, within and through the agency of his total organism, a partitive condition that is common to the species man. This is the integral function of the organism that was forfeited by us when, as infants, we assimilated the partitive, divisive mood of the parental "I"-persona with its spurious dichotomy of right and wrong. (1950)[11]

My associates and I recognize, of course, that in our group approach to the problem of behavior we have made but a beginning, and a very meager beginning. We recognize too that even this meager beginning of an understanding of social man must abort in mere futility unless there is the cooperation and participation of scientists the world over in defining and accepting the larger biological pattern of behavior native to man as a social organism. I assure you that we have no illusions as to our limitations as a special experimental unit or group. For a long time we have fully realized that no single group, no restricted section of the social community, can perform a task which, of its nature, belongs to the species. The scientist who studies infectious disease or cancer does not restrict his investigations to a single group or community.

Neither can the scientist who studies the forces and relations that determine human behavior adopt a parochial attitude toward his problem. Science, like art, is a universal language. It is necessary that scientists everywhere recognize and impart to the wider community of man the global nature of his behavioral conflict. Tackling the behavior of the human species is indeed a large order. But it is one that belongs to scientists the world over as well as to ourselves. (1950)[12]

At this point one might well ask: "Assuming that your position is correct, just how is the patient—that is, the sick society of man—to be induced to accept the prescription? What is to persuade him to swallow so unpalatable a dose of behavioral medicine?"

This is indeed a question that requires looking into. As a science of subjective man—a science that deals with processes within us—phylobiology is of its nature a discipline applicable equally to scientist and layman. But for both scientist and layman it must be emphasized that only a mature interest in improved methods of human adaptation—only a passionate interest in the organism's fullest measure of balanced function and health—can possibly incite a student to pit his organismic self against the self of automatic habit. In substance, his problem is to exercise the scientific discipline that will give precedence to the delayed reaction in contrast to the immediate response, even where the adjustment will affect his entire personality with all its agelong entail of reflex habituations. Certainly nothing could be more unacceptable to him in the entire pharmacopeia of behavior remedies than a recipe for undermining all that he now knows as his personality, and adopting instead a procedure that will insure a total (phylic) pattern of reaction of which he has as yet no conscious knowledge.

To the student who has not participated in the technique of phylobiology, the situation may look rather hopeless. But from my own experience and that of others, it is by no means hopeless. When man *must* do something, he finds a way to do it. Today it is not only the biologist, the sociologist, the philosopher, the psychologist and the economist who are concerned with the signs in man of social imbalance and disintegration; people everywhere are hard pressed to reconcile the inconsistencies in our human behavior with a sane program of individual and social adaptation. People are daily becoming increasingly aware of serious difficulty, of pain and impediment, for which they cannot account. As a consequence, I believe that the habit mechanisms of affect, prejudice and projection will be brought more and more under scrutiny, and that intelligent folk on each side of this divided and unhappy world will demand of themselves the discipline of an inquiry that offers a radical challenge to the accepted behavior precepts prevailing throughout the processes of us all.

I do not doubt that the needed social discipline, which in our experimental group work came to be exerted upon my associates and myself, will gradually come to exert itself spontaneously over the processes of human beings, in sufficient numbers and with sufficient strength to give the lie to the behavioral prescriptions—religious, political, ethical, legal, educational— now accepted among us as *bona fide* remedies for a disorder of adaptation which man will in spite of himself be forced to recognize as a *physiological disturbance internal to him*. With the increasing opportunities of contact between individuals and nations, with the closer interknitting physically of men and institutions the world over, there is an intimation, however vague, however inchoate, of a corresponding trend within the processes of men toward recognizing, beneath the clash of our superficial ideologies, the essentially common nature of persons and peoples throughout the human family.

Man's present-day institutions, however, do not reflect this phylobiological trend. In the false, unilateral ideology of so-called communism, there is no hint, no faint intimation, of such an inherent biological coordination and unity. And in the surface pictures of the systems supposedly representative of the people, in the so-called democracies, there is likewise no basic correspondence with the primary oneness of feeling and motivation intrinsic to man as a solidaric species. From the more inclusive viewpoint, the democracies are also unilateral. In their present forms both communism and democracy are but a symbol and a forecast. None of these reactions of social man bears any true relation to the organismic solidarity of the species. Hence it is useless to argue from an ideological premise. Verbal (symbolic) interchange does not touch the distorted mood that is responsible for man's ideological hostilities.

Man has need of a deeper, basic consciousness, a consciousness consistent with his essential continuity as a race. Reason cannot operate as long as man continues to violate so essential a principle as that of the solidarity of the species. (1950)[13]

Mankind is in the grip of a vast mood-contagion. We are like the distraught community described by Dostoevsky in the prophetic dream of Raskolnikov:

He dreamt that the whole world was condemned to a

terrible new strange plague that had come to Europe
from the depths of Asia . . . Some new sorts of microbes
were endowed with intelligence and will. Men at-
tacked by them at once became mad and furious. But
never had men considered themselves so intellectual
and so completely in possession of the truth as these
sufferers, never had they considered their decisions,
their scientific conclusions, their moral convictions so
infallible. Whole villages, whole towns and peoples
went mad from the infection. All were excited and did
not understand one another. Each thought that he
alone had the truth and was wretched looking at the
others . . . They did not know how to judge and could
not agree what to consider evil and what good; they did
not know whom to blame, whom to justify . . . They
gathered together in armies against one another, but
even on the march the armies would begin attacking
one another, the ranks would be broken and the soldiers
would fall on each other. The alarm bell was ringing all
day long in the towns; men rushed together, but why
they were summoned and who was summoning them
no one knew. The most ordinary trades were abandoned, because everyone proposed his own ideas, his
own improvements, and they could not agree. The land
too was abandoned. Men met in groups, agreed on
something, swore to keep together, but at once began
on something quite different from what they had proposed. They accused one another, fought and killed
each other. There were conflagrations and famine. All
men and all things were involved in destruction. The
plague spread and moved further and further. Only a
few men could be saved in the whole world.

Today, in his separate mood of arbitrary rightness, man
is mad. As he goes on with his image patchwork and
clings tenaciously to the detached and divisive symbol, there is approximated ever more closely a state of
world-wide behavioral conflict and neurosis such as

that envisaged in the prescient dream of Dostoevsky's hero. In the issues of today, debate has reached an impasse. Like the people in Raskolnikov's dream, we shall turn on and destroy one another unless science steps in and single-mindedly focuses on an objective consideration of this conflict of *my* right versus *your* right—a conflict that is at this very moment confounding the intelligent processes of mankind. The time has come for decisive, disinterested analysis. (1964)[14]

There is required throughout the world the establishment of groups of behavior students bent upon a strictly physiological technique of behavior-adjustment. Out of the work of such groups will grow a science, a recognized world authority in human behavior. Like the cancer experts, such groups will be interested in healing disorders throughout the organism of man. They will not be interested in modifying the behavior of a particular person, clique, political party or country. They will know that the healing of the phylosoma will alone bring healing to the ontosoma. In applying the function of their whole brain and senses to the larger problem of human behavior, they will embody a world confederacy of cotention or of common feeling and thinking. From this common organismic background they will welcome in common the recognition of whatever ditentive or deviate reactions, whether occurring in themselves or others, tend to obstruct the unified function of the whole—of man as a total phylic organism.

From this cotentive premise they will make clear to the world that their feeling and motivation rests upon full scientific authority, upon a principle of organismic balance and solidarity. They will not truckle to the partitive machinations of political demagogues.

The position of these investigators will be: "We are one people, one world, one organism. We will not fight your wars, we will not go to your election polls, we will not take part in political and social conflicts. We will have no patriotism in the narrow, partitive sense of the word. But in all that pertains to man, you can count on us. And you can count on us not to violate the principle of man's biological solidarity as a species." (1949)[15]

It is, of course, not within my province to offer suggestions as to ways and means of establishing such a scientific federation of individuals and peoples. But from my experience in group- or phyloanalysis I feel strongly the need for the organization of a generic state based upon inclusive, scientific principles, as contrasted with regional states based upon affective, political differences. For as things stand, individuals and peoples are ruthlessly destroying both themselves and the natural resources of their environment under the prevailing sovereignty of a partitive premise of adaptation. There is the need of some such biologically homogeneous state in order to guarantee the very survival of man. We need to establish a world state in which scientists and laymen are organized not to fight one another, but to fight the archenemy of all states and all peoples—the spurious, dissociative "I"-persona now besetting the balanced behavior of man as a phyloorganism.

In this day, in this hour of acute social crisis, we must approach the problem of human behavior from a wholly altered frame of reference. It is the obligation of a scientific gathering such as this* to secure a world

---

* *The Mooseheart Symposium on Feelings and Emotions* (1950) attended by investigators in a number of scientific disciplines.-Ed.

federation, an international organization that rests upon a phyloorganismic basis. An organization of political and economic delegates can no more reach and remedy the physiological disfunction responsible for a subversive mood in man than it can reach and remedy the pathogenic factors responsible for poliomyelitis. This problem is not one for politicians, for industrialists, or for world reformers. It is not the statesman, not the clergyman, not the educator, not the psychiatric practioner, who can aid us. All these are *inter*relational in their approach. Man's condition is essentially *intra*relational. The lesion from which man suffers is within the organism of man.

This internal lesion is our problem. It is the problem of the men and women who are here today and whose colleagues are distributed throughout the world—men and women who have proved their competence and authority in varied fields of investigation. It is we who, in respect to man's social behavior, must take over what is ours, namely, the scientific understanding and formulation of the basic cause of man's world-wide disharmonies. It devolves upon us to remove the problem of human behavior from the entire field of tradition and speculation—from religion, as now understood, from morality and other supernatural instrumentalities—and make plain to ourselves and to the community that the understanding and control of disordered behavior processes is a discipline that lies within the category of the biophysical sciences. We must compass at last the neurodynamic disfunction embodied in neurosis and war, just as the scientist has compassed the understanding and cure of somatic disturbance in the organism of the single individual. (1950)[16]

Granting the possibility that the bionomic thesis which has emerged from our researches becomes accepted by a few people here and there throughout the world, one can readily predict an increased social eagerness to recognize and set aside diseased behavioral processes that are now responsible for the universal phenomenon of human conflict. In this eventuality there would automatically come to pass the acceptance of the internal principle of species solidarity as the one basic law governing the behavior of organismic man. While in the small group comprising The Lifwynn Laboratory there are today only the first stirrings of an awareness of this internal constant—of this central principle of behavior and its conscious correlation with the processes inherent in the world of external phenomena—even these first faint inklings give evidence of its overmastering power, its irresistible sovereignty over man's motivation and behavior as an organism.

Under the clarifying influence of a general recognition that the problems of man's behavior are basically physiological and phylic problems, there will be quite spontaneously a world-wide resurgence of those basic cotentive values and capacities that make for organismic communication and production. Only then will we recognize that it is governments that are the chief obstacle to government; that it is the artificial supremacy we now give to the part-function of man's brain that precludes the operation of man's orderly brain-function as a whole. Today governments are going to pieces on every hand. Governments will continue to go to pieces until they have recognized that they are subjugated to the "I"-persona, that their policies are subjective, not objective, that they are animated solely by self-interest and prejudice, that they lack an inclusive or total basis of motivation and aim.

True government embodies a total autonomic process. In the absence of total, autonomic government, there is no government. There is only tyranny— tyranny over oneself as well as over others. Partitive governments must at last give way to total government. Only then will we have begun to banish from the face of the earth the discriminations and prejudices that rest upon mere superficial differences—differences of color, creed and of merely conditioned habits of adaptation. Then only will the real likenesses, the truly common or organismic identities among human beings begin to be felt—identities of structure and function based upon common neural and muscular systems, common biological needs, organismically common and indivisible reactions to a common and indivisible environment. In some such world wide confederacy, our cruel barriers—ethnological, political and religious—will be wiped away. The life of man will be motivated and governed by a broad organismic economy, and the narrow incitements of political self-interest and unilateralism will no longer have a place in the sun. (1949)[17]

Source Notes

[1] *The Neurosis of Man*, p. 269
[2] *Ibid.*, p. 292
[3] *Ibid.*, p. 179
[4] *Ibid.*, pp. 189–90
[5] *Ibid.*, pp. 21–22
[6] "The Social Neurosis," p. 32
[7] *The Neurosis of Man*, pp. xxv–xxvi
[8] *Ibid.*, pp. 22–23
[9] *Ibid.*, p. 334
[10] *The Biology of Human Conflict*, p. 8
[11] "Emotion and the Social Crisis," p. 478
[12] *Ibid.*, p. 482
[13] "Prescription for Peace," pp. 112–14
[14] *Preconscious Foundations of Human Experience*, pp. 142–43
[15] *The Neurosis of Man*, pp. 344–45
[16] "Emotion and the Social Crisis," pp. 484–86
[17] *The Neurosis of Man*, pp. 345–47

Glossary*

Affect: A reaction that is subjectively biased through the artificial linkage of feeling and symbol, leading to imbalance and distortion of interrelational behavior. (Synonyms: autopathic feeling, partitive feeling. Contrasted with primary, total feeling.)

Affecto-symbolic: Type of behavior characterized by mental bias. (See *Ditentive*. Contrasted with cotentive.)

Autopathic: Feeling that has been distorted by self-consciousness and bias. (See *Ditentive*.)

Cerebro-ocular: Behavior-reactions involving combined function of brain and organ of vision.

Cotention, Cotentive: The type of attention that marks the organism's total tensional reaction in relation to the environment, and that precludes the usual play of wishful fantasies with their interrelational affects and strivings. (Contrasted with ditention.)

Ditention, Ditentive: The intrusion of affect-elements or bias into ordinary attention. Ditention is a reaction that characterizes man's interrelational behavior generally. (Contrasted with cotention.)

Ecosomatic: Variant of term "organism-environment."

---

* Based on glossaries in *The Neurosis of Man* and *The Biology of Human Conflict*, both by Trigant Burrow.

151

"I"-persona: The restricted part-expression of the personality, or the affective identity through which man, individual and social, achieves his symbolic interchange. The "I"-persona represents the systematized sum of the individual's projective, symbolic processes with their divisive "feelings" or affects, in contrast to the primary coordination of function motivating the behavior of the organism as a whole. (Synonyms: "I"-complex, social substantive "I." Contrasted with total organism.)

Neurodynamics: Term used by the author in connection with investigations which posit the thesis that the interrelational disorders of man are due to disturbance in the organism's internal tensional patterns.

Ontosoma: The single individual or element of a species. From the background of phylobiology the individual is viewed as an integrated unit within the phylic whole. (See also *Phyloorganism, Phylosoma.*)

Partitive: Characterizing the intrusion of inappropriate symbolic elements into the primary empathic zone of the total organism, leading to distortion and segmentation of whole feeling. (Synonym: Affective.)

Phylic: Referring to man as a species. (Synonyms: generic, racial, phyloorganismic, phylosomatic. Contrasted with individual, ontosomatic, social.)

Phyloanalysis: A method developed by the author for investigating disorders in human behavior. Originally called group analysis. Phyloanalysis regards the symptoms of individual and society as but the outer aspect of impaired tensional processes that affect the balance of the organism's internal reaction as a whole. (Synonym: group analysis. Not to be confused with group therapy. From φῦλον, phylum, race.)

Phylobiology: The science of behavior that studies the relation of the organism as a whole in its adaptation to the environment and to other organisms. Phylobiology posits a principle of functional unity and solidarity activating the behavior of individual and species.

Phyloorganism: The species man regarded as an organismic whole in which the element or individual is a phylically integrated unit. (Synonym: phylosoma. See also *Ontosoma.*)

Phylosoma: The species man as a unitary organism. (Synonyms: phyloorganism, phylum. See also *Ontosoma.*)

Phylum: In phylobiology this word is used to include the human race irrespective of ethnological or geographical differentiations. (Synonyms: race, species.)

Preconscious; Primary Identification: The primary phase or mode of consciousness of the infant in which there is complete identification with the mother organism. This preconscious mode represents the nonlibidinal, pre-objective phase of the organism's development. In later life it finds symbolic expression in art, poetry, folklore, religion, in dreams and fantasies. Not to be confused with the psychoanalytic term "preconscious" or "foreconscious."

Social Neurosis: The disorder and conflict existing throughout man's social structure, though universally unrecognized by him. Viewed phylobiologically, the social neurosis is the generic condition of which the individual manifestations of mental and nervous disorders, crime and social conflict are merely symptomatic expressions.

Socio-symbolic: This term refers to the organism's social interchange by means of symbol and speech.

Acknowledgments

Grateful acknowledgment is made to the following publishers and institutions for their permission to use excerpts from the publications designated, all by Trigant Burrow, M.D., Ph.D.:

Basic Books, Inc. for *Preconscious Foundations of Human Experience*, edited by William E. Galt; Foreword by Nathan W. Ackerman. New York: Basic Books, 1964, pp. xxvi, 164.

The British Psychological Society for "The Basis of Group Analysis, or the Analysis of the Reactions of Normal and Neurotic Individuals," *The British Journal of Medical Psychology*, 1928, Vol. 8, pp. 198–206.

Elsevier North Holland, Inc. for "Kymograph Records of Neuromuscular (Respiratory) Patterns in Relation to Behavior Disorders," *Psychosomatic Medicine*, 1941, Vol. 3, pp. 174–86.

Journal Press for "The Organismic Factor in Disorders of Behavior," *The Journal of Psychology*, 1937, Vol. 4, pp. 333–41; and "Neurosis and War: A Problem in Human Behavior," *The Journal of Psychology*, 1941, Vol. 12, pp. 235–49.

The Orthological Institute for "The Autonomy of the 'I' from the Standpoint of Group Analysis," *Psyche* (London), 1928, Vol. 8, pp. 35–50; and for "Physiological Behavior-Reactions in the Individual and the Community: A Study in Phyloanalysis," *Psyche* (London), 1930, Vol. 11, pp. 67–81.

Oxford University Press for *A Search for Man's Sanity: The Selected Letters of Trigant Burrow with Biographical Notes,* edited by the Editorial Committee of The Lifwynn Foundation, William E. Galt, Chairman. Foreword by Sir Herbert Read. New York: Oxford University Press, 1958, pp. xxi, 615.

Philosophical Library for *The Neurosis of Man: An Introduction to a Science of Human Behavior,* London: Routledge and Kegan Paul; New York: Harcourt, Brace and Company, 1950, pp. xxvi, 428; and *Science and Man's Behavior: The Contribution of Phylobiology,* (including the full text of *The Neurosis of Man*) edited by William E. Galt, New York: Philosophical Library, 1953, pp. 564.

Sergei P. Sorokin, M.D., for "Prescription for Peace: The Biological Basis of Man's Ideological Conflicts," in *Explorations in Altruistic Love and Behavior,* edited by Pitirim A. Sorokin. Boston: The Beacon Press, 1950, pp. 93–117. Reprinted 1970 by Kraus Reprint Company, Millwood, New York.

Williams and Wilkins Company for "The Social Neurosis: A Study in Clinical Anthropology," *Philosophy of Science,* 1949, Vol. 16, pp. 25–40.

Bibliography
Trigant Burrow, M.D., Ph.D.
(1875–1950)

Books

Preconscious Foundations of Human Experience, Edited by William E. Galt, Ph.D. Foreword by Nathan W. Ackerman, M.D. New York: Basic Books, 1964, pp. xxvi, 164·

Science and Man's Behavior: The Contribution of Phylobiology. (Including the full text of *The Neurosis of Man.*) Edited by William E. Galt, Ph.D. New York: Philosophical Library, 1953, pp. 564.
(Reprint edition by Greenwood Press, Westport, Conn., 1968.)

The Neurosis of Man: An Introduction to a Science of Human Behavior. London: Routledge and Kegan Paul; New York: Harcourt, Brace and Co., 1950, pp. xxvi, 428.
(Translation) *A Neurose do Homem.* Belo Horizonte, Brazil: Livraria Itatiaia Editora Ltda, 1974, pp. 474.

The Biology of Human Conflict: An Anatomy of Behavior Individual and Social. Foreword by Clarence Shields. New York: Macmillan Co., 1937, pp. xl, 435.
(Reprint edition by Arno Press, New York, 1974.)

The Structure of Insanity: A Study in Phylopathology. Psyche Miniatures. London: Kegan Paul, Trench, Trubner and Co., 1932, pp. 80.
(Translation) *Die Struktur der Geisteskrankheit: Eine Studie in Phylopathologie.* Translated by Miriam Bredow. Leipzig: Georg Thieme, 1933, pp. 52.

The Social Basis of Consciousness: A Study in Organic Psychology. The International Library of Psychology, Philosophy and Scientific Method. New York: Harcourt, Brace and Co.; London: Kegan Paul, Trench, Trubner and Co., 1927, pp. xviii, 256.

A Search for Man's Sanity: The Selected Letters of Trigant Burrow with Biographical Notes. Editorial Committee of The Lifwynn Foundation, William E. Galt, Ph.D., Chairman. Foreword by Sir Herbert Read. New York: Oxford University Press, 1958, pp. xxi, 615.
(Reprint edition by Arno Press, New York, 1979.)

Papers

Prescription for Peace: The Biological Basis of Man's Ideological Conflicts. In *Explorations in Altruistic Love and Behavior,* edited by Pitirim A. Sorokin. Boston: The Beacon Press, 1950, pp. 93–117.
(Published in abbreviated form in *Man and International Relations,* edited by J. K. Zawodny, Vol. 2, Integration. San Francisco: Chandler Publishing Co., 1966, pp. 729–38.)

Emotion and the Social Crisis: A Problem in Phylobiology. In *Feelings and Emotions: The Mooseheart Symposium,* edited by Martin L. Reymert. New York: McGraw-Hill Book Co., 1950, pp. 465–86.

Studies with the Lifwynn Eye-Movement Camera (with Hans Syz). *Journal of the Biological Photographic Association,* 1949, Vol. 17, pp. 155–70.

Two Modes of Social Adaptation and Their Concomitants in Ocular Movements (with Hans Syz). *The Journal of Abnormal and Social Psychology,* 1949, Vol. 44, pp. 191–211.

The Social Neurosis: A Study in "Clinical Anthropology." *Philosophy of Science,* 1949, Vol. 16, pp. 25–40.
(Japanese translation) **The Social Neurosis.** *Tokyo Jour-*

nal of Psychoanalysis, 1956, Vol. 14, pp. 1–9.

Phylobiology: Behavior Reactions in the Individual and the Community. *ETC.*, 1946, Vol. 3, pp. 265–78.
(Previously published under the title, Physiological Behavior-Reactions in the Individual and the Community. *Psyche*, 1930, Vol. 11, pp. 67–81.)

Electroencephalographic Recordings of Varying Aspects of Attention in Relation to Behavior (with William E. Galt). *The Journal of General Psychology*, 1945, Vol. 32, pp. 269–88.

The Neurodynamics of Behavior: A Phylobiological Foreword. *Philosophy of Science*, 1943, Vol. 10, pp. 271–88.

Preliminary Report of Electroencephalographic Recordings in Relation to Behavior Modifications. *The Journal of Psychology*, 1943, Vol. 15, pp. 109–14.

Neurosis and War: A Problem in Human Behavior. *The Journal of Psychology*, 1941, Vol. 12, pp. 235–49.

Kymograph Records of Neuromuscular (Respiratory) Patterns in Relation to Behavior Disorders. *Psychosomatic Medicine*, 1941, Vol. 3, pp. 174–86.

The Human Equation. *Mental Hygiene*, 1941, Vol. 25, pp. 210–20.

The Economic Factor in Disorders of Behavior. *The American Journal of Orthopsychiatry*, 1939, Vol. 9, pp. 102–08.

The World as Will: A View and a Review. *Journal of Social Philosophy*, 1939, Vol. 4, pp. 162–73.

Kymograph Studies of Physiological (Respiratory) Concomitants in Two Types of Attentional Adaptation. *Nature* (London), 1938, Vol. 142, pp. 156–57.

Bio-Physical Factors in Relation to Functional Imbalances. *Human Biology*, 1938, Vol. 10, pp. 93–105.

The Lifwynn Foundation: An Organismic Study of Behavior in the Individual and in the Community. *Transactions of The New York Academy of Sciences*, 1938, Vol. 1, pp. 25–28.

The Organism as a Whole and its Phyloanalytic Implications: An Organismic Approach to Disorders of Human Behavior. *The Australasian Journal of Psychology and Philosophy*, 1937, Vol. 15, pp. 259–78.

The Organismic Factor in Disorders of Behavior. *The Journal of Psychology*, 1937, Vol. 4, pp. 333–41.

The Law of the Organism: A Neuro-Social Approach to the Problems of Human Behavior. *The American Journal of Sociology*, 1937, Vol. 42, pp. 814–24.

Altering Frames of Reference in the Sphere of Human Behavior. *Journal of Social Philosophy*, 1937, Vol. 2, pp. 118–41.

Fallacies of the Senses. *"Scientia,"* 1935, Vol. 57, Part 1, pp. 354–65; Part 2, pp. 431–41.
(Translation) Illusions des Sens. Supplement to *"Scientia,"* 1935, Vol. 57, Première Partie, pp. 117–28; Deuxième Partie, pp. 153–62.

Behavior Mechanisms and Their Phylopathology. *The Psychoanalytic Review*, 1935, Vol. 22, pp. 169–81.

Neuropathology and the Internal Environment: A Study of the Neuromuscular Factors in Attention and Their Bearing upon Man's Disorders of Adaptation. *Human Biology*, 1935, Vol. 7, pp. 74–94.

The Morphology of Insanity as a Racial Process: A Study of Attention in Relation to Adaptive Disorders. *The British Journal of Medical Psychology*, 1933, Vol. 13, pp. 296–312.

Crime and the Social Reaction of Right and Wrong: A Study in Clinical Sociology. *Journal of Criminal Law and Criminology*, 1933, Vol. 24, pp. 685–99.

(Translation) **Le crime et la force sociale de la notion du bien et du mal:** étude clinique de sociologie, *Revue Internationale de Droit Pénal*, 1935, Vol. 12, pp. 265–84.

A Phylogenetic Study of Insanity in its Underlying Morphology. *The Journal of the American Medical Association*, 1933, Vol. 100, pp. 648–51.
(Translation) **Uno studio filogenetico della alienazione mentale e delle sue basi morfologiche.** *Archivio Generale di Neurologia Psichiatria e Psicoanalisi,* 1934, Vol. 15, pp. 133–42.

Physiological Behavior-Reactions in the Individual and the Community: A Study in Phyloanalysis. *Psyche* (London), 1930, Vol. 11, pp. 67–81.
(Translations) **Physiologische Verhaltensreaktionen im Individuum und in der Gesellschaft:** Eine Studie in Phyloanalyse. *Schweizer Archiv für Neurologie und Psychiatrie*, 1932, Vol. 29, pp. 253–68.
Réactions physiologiques du comportement individuel et collectif: Une étude en phyloanalyse. *Journal de Neurologie et de Psychiatrie*, 1932, Vol. 32, pp. 442–59.

So-called "Normal" Social Relationships Expressed in the Individual and the Group, and their Bearing on the Problems of Neurotic Disharmonies. *The American Journal of Psychiatry*, 1930, Vol. 10, pp. 101–16.
(Translation) **Sogenannte "normale" soziale Wechselbeziehungen in Individuum und Gruppe und ihre Bedeutung für das Problem neurotischer Störungen.** *Zentralblatt für Psychotherapie und ihre Grenzgebiete*, 1932, Vol. 5, pp. 677–91.

The Physiological Basis of Neurosis and Dream: A Societal Interpretation of the Sensori-Motor Reactions Reflected in Insanity and Crime. *The Journal of Social Psychology*, 1930, Vol. 1, pp. 48–65.
(Translation) **Über Phylopathologie und Phyloanalyse:** Eine physiologische Deutung der gestörten sozialen Interreaktionen. *Zentralblatt für Psychotherapie und ihre Grenzgebiete*, 1930, Vol. 3, pp. 394–411.

The Autonomy of the "I" from the Standpoint of Group Analysis. *Psyche.* (London), 1928, Vol. 8, pp. 35–50.

Biological Foundations and Mental Methods. *The British Journal of Medical Psychology,* 1928, Vol. 8, pp. 49–63.

The Basis of Group-Analysis, or the Analysis of the Reactions of Normal and Neurotic Individuals. *The British Journal of Medical Psychology,* 1928, Vol. 8, pp. 198–206.

The Problem of the Transference. *The British Journal of Medical Psychology,* 1927, Vol. 7, pp. 193–202.

The Group Method of Analysis. *The Psychoanalytic Review,* 1927, Vol. 14, pp. 268–80. (Published also in *Group Psychotherapy and Group Function,* edited by Max Rosenbaum and Milton Berger. New York: Basic Books, 1963, pp. 154–61.)
(Translation) **Die Gruppenmethode in der Psychoanalyse.** *Imago,* 1926, Vol. 12, pp. 211–22.

Speaking of Resistances. *Psyche* (London), 1927, Vol. 7, pp. 20–27.

An Ethnic Aspect of Consciousness. *The Sociological Review* (London), 1927, Vol. 19, pp. 69–76.

The Need of an Analytic Psychiatry. *The American Journal of Psychiatry,* 1927, Vol. 6, pp. 485–92.

The Reabsorbed Affect and its Elimination. *The British Journal. of Medical Psychology,* 1926, Vol. 6, pp. 209–18.

Psychoanalysis in Theory and in Life. *The Journal of Nervous and Mental Disease,* 1926, Vol. 64, pp. 209–24.

The Heroic Role: An Historical Retrospect. *Psyche* (London), 1926, Vol. 6, pp. 42–54.

Insanity a Social Problem. *The American Journal of Sociology,* 1926, Vol. 32, pp. 80–87.

Our Social Evasion. *Medical Journal and Record*, 1926, Vol. 123, pp. 793–96.

Our Mass Neurosis. *The Psychological Bulletin*, 1926, Vol. 23, pp. 305–12.

Psychoanalytic Improvisations and the Personal Equation. *The Psychoanalytic Review*, 1926, Vol. 13, pp. 173–86.

The Laboratory Method in Psychoanalysis: Its Inception and Development. *The American Journal of Psychiatry*, 1926, Vol. 5, pp. 345–55.
(Translation) **Die Laboratoriumsmethode in der Psychoanalyse:** Ihr Anfang und ihre Entwicklung. *Internationale Zeitschrift für Psychoanalyse*, 1928, Vol. 14, pp. 375–86.

Penny Wise and Pound Foolish. *Mental Health*, 1926, Vol. 3, No. 7, pp. 1–4.

Psychiatry as an Objective Science. *The British Journal of Medical Psychology*, 1925, Vol. 5, pp. 298–309.

A Relative Concept of a Consciousness: An Analysis of Consciousness in its Ethnic Origin. *The Psychoanalytic Review*, 1925, Vol. 12, pp. 1–15.

The Camera Man. *The Survey*, 1925, Vol. 14, pp. 517–37.

Social Images versus Reality. *The Journal of Abnormal Psychology and Social Psychology*, 1924, Vol. 19, pp. 230–35.

1920 and earlier
(Prior to group analytic studies)

The Origin of the Incest-Awe. *The Psychoanalytic Review*, 1918, Vol. 5, pp. 243–54 (Published also in *Preconscious Foundations of Human Experience*. New York: Basic Books, 1964, pp. 23–38.)

Notes with Reference to Freud, Jung and Adler. *The Journal of Abnormal Psychology*, 1917, Vol. 12, pp. 161–67.

The Genesis and Meaning of "Homosexuality" and its Relation to the Problem of Introverted Mental States. *The Psychoanalytic Review,* 1917, Vol. 4, pp. 272–84.

The Meaning of Psychoanalysis. *The Journal of Abnormal Psychology,* 1917, Vol. 12, pp. 58–68.

Conceptions and Misconceptions in Psychanalysis. *The Journal of the American Medical Association,* 1917, Vol. 68, pp. 355–60. (Published also in *Contemporary Science,* edited by Benjamin Harrow. New York: Boni and Liveright, 1921, pp. 211–29.)

Permutations within the Sphere of Consciousness; or, the Factor of Repression and its Influence upon Education. *The Journal of Abnormal Psychology,* 1916, Vol. 11, pp. 178–88.

The Philology of Hysteria: An a Priori Study of the Neuroses in the Light of Freudian Psychology. *The Journal of the American Medical Association,* 1916, Vol. 66, pp. 783–87.

The Psychanalyst and the Community. *The Journal of the American Medical Association,* 1914, Vol. 62, pp. 1876–78.

Character and the Neuroses. *The Psychoanalytic Review,* 1914, Vol. 1, pp. 121–28.

The Meaning of the Psychic Factor. *The Journal of Abnormal Psychology,* 1913–14, Vol. 8, pp. 3–11.

The Psychological Analysis of So-called Neurasthenic and Allied States: A Fragment. *The Journal of Abnormal Psychology,* 1913, Vol. 8, pp. 243–58.
(Translation) **Die psychologische Analyse der sogenannten Neurasthenie und verwandter Zustände.** *Internationale Zeitschrift für ärztliche Psychoanalyse,* 1913, Vol. 1, pp. 330–43.

The Method of Psychoanalysis. *The Virginia Medical Semi-Monthly,* 1913, Vol. 18, pp. 430–33.

The Psychotherapeutic Treatment of the Functional Neuroses (with L. F. Barker). *Therapeusis of Internal Diseases*, edited by F. Forchheimer. New York: Appleton, 1913, Vol. 4, pp. 569–81.

Psychoanalysis and Society. *The Journal of Abnormal Psychology*, 1912–13, Vol. 7, pp. 340–46.

Conscious and Unconscious Mentation from the Psychoanalytic Viewpoint. *Psychological Bulletin*, 1912, Vol. 9, pp. 154–60.

Some Psychological Phases of Medicine. *The Journal of Abnormal Psychology*, 1911, Vol. 6, pp. 205–13.

Freud's Psychology in its Relation to the Neuroses. *American Journal of the Medical Sciences*, 1911, Vol. 141, pp. 873–82.

Hysterical Defects of Musical Language. *Maryland Medical Journal*, 1909, Vol. 52, pp. 249–50.

The Determination of the Position of a Momentary Impression in the Temporal Course of a Moving Visual Impression. Doctoral thesis. The Johns Hopkins Studies in Philosophy and Psychology. No. 3. *The Psychological Review: Psychological Monographs*, 1909, Vol. 11, pp. 1–63.

Index

Ackerman, Nathan W., xi–xiv
Aeschylus, 17
affect, 26, 34, 41, 44, 71–72, 80,
   91; images, elimination of,
   87–88, 100–01, 129; one's
   own, 91, 100–01, 129–30;
   projection, 49
Allee, W. C., 6 fn
American Psychoanalytic
   Assn., xi, xxi
anger, 49–50
anthropology, applied, 137
apraxia, social, 120
Arnold, Matthew, 17
art, 17
atomic energy, 138–39
attention, 79–83; deflection of,
   xxiii, 59, 63–67; an ecological
   process, 81–82; neuromuscular substrate of, 86; organic
   mode of, 9–10. See also cotention; ditention

behavior, 12–13, 16, 30, 61 fn,
   64–65, 68, 76, 120; disordered, 16, 66 fn, 74, 76, 136,
   142, 147; organismic principle of, 7–8; a physiological
   problem, 15–16, 19, 27, 119;
   primary pattern of, 9–10, 56–
   58, 61 fn; 68, 118; a science
   of, 135–36, 137, 145–46. See

also "normality"; organism
   of man
Berne, Eric, xi
Bertalanffy, Ludwig von, xxxi,
   53 fn
Beukenkamp, Cornelius, xi
Bohm, David, 12 fn*
bonds, organic, 3, 5. *See also*
   unity, inherent
brain, 66–67, 105, 148; disorder
   in, 70–72, 72–73, projective
   function of, 70–73; symbolic
   segment, 58, 86, 127; third,
   61 fn*
brain waves, 110–11, 113–14
Brill, A. A., xviii
Burrow, Trigant, vii–xxxi; education and professional experience, xviii; frame of
   reference, xvi–xvii, 1, 25,
   role-reversal with analysand,
   ix–x, xx, xxxv–xxxviii, 27–28;
   writings, ix–xxxix passim, 22,
   79, 110

Cannon, Walter B., xiii
Carlson, A. J., 12
child, 53–56, 59, 63–67
Coghill, George E., 61 fn**
communication, xxiii, 3, 10;
   shift upward, 59
communism, 143

167

competitiveness, 18. *See also*
conflict; division
conditioning, social, 33–34, 40,
68
conflict, 12–13, 38, 62; in animal species, 18; industrial,
27; internal nature of, 49, 139;
physiological, 74, 85. *See also*
competitiveness; division
consciousness, xv–xvi, 2, 100;
organic principle of, 6; and
physiology, xxii, 25–26; need
of a basic, 143; primary pattern of, 58; societal, 31. *See
also* attention
Cooney, James P.: letter to,
125
cotention, xxiii–xxiv, 14, 79, 83–
84, 85–100, 104–05, 123, 126,
128; analagy to swimming,
97–99; a criterion of health,
74–75, 92, 99–100; and disease, 93; and drugs, 118; eye-
movements in, 110; and
learning, 92; not a mental
function, 102–03, 124, 127,
129; physiological changes
in, 109–11, 115–16; a social
process, 117, 130. *See also*
norm, biological; phylobiological technique
cotentive function, 87–88, 92–
93, 99–100, 148
cotentive technique. *See* phylobiological technique
cowardice, 124
crime, xxx, 27, 53

Darwin, Charles, 4
democracies, the, 143

ditention, xxiii, 67, 75, 79, 83–
89, 99–101, 129; and the eyes,
85–87, 101–02; and fantasy,
101; instrumental studies in,
109–10, 113; not problem of
individual, 105, 121; a secondary pattern, 92
division, 10–11, 21, 34, 94; universality of, 14–16. *See also*
conflict
Dostoevsky, Feodor, 143

ecology. *See* organism/environ-
ment relationship
economic disorders, 19, 27
ego, 48
ego-sexuality, xxx
elation/depression, 96, 136
electroencephalograms (EEG).
See brain waves
Eliot, Thomas D.: letter to, 32
"Environmental Forces"
(Lewin), 63 fn
exteroceptive action pattern,
60–61, 84
"Extraorganic, The" (Greenman), 67 fn*
eye-movements, 112–13; in cotention, 110
eye, 84–85; and convergence,
109; steadied, 88–90, 96, 114.
See also ocular musculature;
tensions, physiological, and
the eyes

face-saving, 62
fall of man, 20
fantasy, 45, 101
faux pas, developmental, 49, 69,
82–83

Federn, Paul: letter to, 31
feeling, 8, 60, 62–63, 73, 123, 126; phylic, 73; substrate, 32–33; symbol attachment, 53
freedom, 58
Freud, Sigmund, xv, xviii, 12–13, 31

Galt, Alfreda: letters to, 120, 128
Galt, William E.: letters to, 17, 94, 126
Goldstein, Kurt, xxxi
government, 19–20, 148–49
Greenman, E. F., 67 fn*
group, 4–6, 117–18, 120; organism, 47–48; physiological processes of, xxii–xxiii, 119–20
group analysis, viii fn, x, xxxi, xxiv–xxviii, 7, 13–14, 20, 27–28, 117 fn; of the group by the group, 30–31. *See also* phyloanalysis
group encounter, xxvi, 25
group therapy, xx–xxi, 25, 31–32, 76

Head, Henry, 46
health, basic, 69. *See* norm, biological
Heard, Gerald, 6 fn
here/now orientation. *See* immediate moment
Herrick, C. Judson, 11
homeostasis, 21, 67, 136; and cotention, 92
Hound of Heaven (Thompson), 17

"I"/"me," 27, 36–37, 119, 122–23
"I"-persona, 26, 36–39, 47–48, 60, 63, 73, 89, 135–36; and attention, 82; and dictators, 42; defense of, 47; and prejudice, 39
immediate moment, xxv–xxvi, 27, 32, 138
individual/society, 1, 6–8, 117, 121
individual/species, 8–9, 49, 73, 124–25, 130, 135
institutions, 21
instrumental studies, xxiv, xxviii, 107–11, 116–17; instructions to subjects, 114
integration, 92, 95, 100
integration, principle of, 21–22
"internal experimentalists," 30, 34, 76, 136
intrarelational disfunction, 49, 74, 147. *See also* social neurosis

Jacobson, Edmund, 112 fn
James-Lange Theory, xxii
Job, Book of, 17
Jung, C. G., xv, xviii, xxx
Kluckhohn, Clyde, 12
Korzybski, Alfred, xxxi, 53 fn
Krishnamurti, 118
Kropotkin, P., 6

language, 55–56. *See also* symbol
Lawrence, D. H., ix, xv
learning, 63–64, 92
Lewin, Kurt, 63 fn
Lifwynn Camp, x, xxiv

Lifwynn Foundation, x, xx,
    xxvii, 119
Lifwynn Laboratory, 105, 107,
    116, 138, 140, 148

madness, human, 11, 145. See
    also social neurosis
male/female, xxix–xxx
meaning, 94
medicine, 9, 19
meditation, 79–80
mental disorder, 11, 14, 27, 136
Meyer, Adolf, xviii; letters to,
    43, 127
mind, somatic nature, xxii
Mirror for Man (Kluckhohn), 12
mood: contagion, 143; inclu-
    sive, 47–48; social, 36-39, 48
motivation, 60, 65–66, 83–84,
    88, 104. See also cotention;
    ditention
Muller, Herbert J., vii-ix
Mutual Aid (Kropotkin), 6 fn

nervous system, 61 fns, 84. See
    also brain
neurobiotaxis, 67 fn
"New Theory of the Neuroses,
    A" (Lawrence), ix, xv
norm, biological, 8–9, 63–65,
    74–76, 92, 136. See also co-
    tention
"normality," 1, 9, 12–14, 20, 32,
    38–39, 101. See also social
    neurosis

Oberndorf, Clarence P., xix
observer's processes, inclusion
    of, xxii–xxiii, 20, 25, 30, 34,
    48, 50, 76, 140. See also "in-
    ternal experimentalists";

phylobiological technique;
    tensions, physiological
ocular musculature, 88–89,
    102, 104. See also tensions,
    physiological
ontosoma/phylosoma, 80, 135,
    145
organism as a whole, 46, 50–51,
    59, 86, 90, 97, 117; physiolog-
    ical bridge to, 95; restoration
    of total sensation, 121–22. See
    also organism of man
organism/environment rela-
    tionship, 9–10, 21, 57–59, 60–
    61, 119; and attention, 81–82;
    and the present, 138; and the
    young, 63–66
organism of man, 2, 8, 21, 57–
    58, 73, 117–18, 120, 135; and
    balance of tensions, 104, 127;
    and basic health, 21, 69; and
    disorder, 15–16, 93–96, 138,
    142; internal impediment,
    139, 147; and language, 59–
    60; and ontoorganism, 103,
    135; a research instrument,
    129, 140; return to biological
    base, 128, 142–43, 147–49;
    self actualization, 128. See
    also species solidarity

pain, 46, 73, 94–95, 129–30;
    mental, 87, 127
parent, 64–67
partitive basis, 14, 30–31, 95.
    See also ditention
pathology, human, 35, 43, 77.
    See also social neurosis
phyloanalysis, viii, 2, 25–33, 37,
    38, 42–49, 109, 138; and af-
    fect, 44–45; material of, 27,

30, 32–33; procedure, 34–35, 44–46; purpose, 4, 29, 39, 46, 120; and self defense, 38, 42–43, 46–47. *See also* group analysis; phylobiological technique

phylobiological research, 4, 26, 33, 48–49, 102–03, 120, 121–22, 133, 141. *See also* phyloanalysis

phylobiological technique, 79–80, 85–90, 96–97, 100–04, 114, 127, 129

phylobiology, 2, 55, 130, 141

phyloorganism, 2, 136; segmentation of, 20, 62. *See also* organism of man

"Phylopathology" (Syz), xii

phylum, 2, 20 30, 135 *See also* organism of man; phyloorganism

physiological basis of function,, 3, 10, 15–16. *See also* tensions, physiological

physiological processes of group, xxii–xxiii

poetry, 17

preconscious mode, ix, xii fn 8, xix fn**, 100

prejudice, 29, 34, 38–39, 41, 136, 149. *See also* affect

prestige, 41, 62

primary identification, principle of. *See* preconscious mode

privilege, 16, 42

projection, 39, 49, 70–73, 105

protoplasm, 8, 136

Prometheus Bound (Aeschylus), 17

psychiatrists, 14, 48

psychoanalysis, xxi–xxii, xxxviii

psychoses, 16

Raskolnikov, dream of, 143–44

Read, Herbert, xii, xv–xvi; letters to, 22, 119–20

"Reflections on War and Death" (Freud), 12

religion, 17

respiration, 109–13, 115

right and wrong, 16, 29, 35–36, 41–43, 64–65, 89; biological, 65

rightness, xvii, 37, 137–38

rights, 69, 137 fn

Russia, 36

Sampter, Jessie: letter to, 118

schizophrenia, 11, 14

science, xxx, 76, 139, 141, 145, 146–47

Science and Criticism (Muller), vii

Seamless Web, The (Burnshaw), xii

self. *See* "I"-persona

self-image, 26, 62. *See also* "I"-persona

self-interest, 18

sensitivity training, 25

sex, xxx, 10, 57

Shaw, George Bernard, 19

Shields, Clarence, xix–xx, xxvii, xxix, xxxviii, 44–45

social images, 7, 45, 86

social neurosis, xviii–xix, 1, 26, 28–29, 38–39, 66, 73; symptoms of, 75, 101. *See also* ditention

social system, 17–18

species, human, 3–4, 12, 15–16, 30. *See also* organism of man

species solidarity, xxxi, 1–9, 69–
  70, 84, 135, 143, 146, 148; and
  cotention, 74, 84. *See also*
  unity, inherent; organism of
  man
species/organismic frame of
  reference, 1, 21, 25, 95
stress. *See* tensions, physiological
students, letters to, 122, 123–25
survival, 18, 104, 146
symbol, ix, 53–56, 58–64, 67–
  68; and attention, 59; and behavior disorder, 66 fn; and
  face, 60, 62; feeling amalgamation with, 60, 101; importance of, 56. *See also* brain,
  symbolic element
Syz, Hans, xii, 44–45

tensional patterns, discrimination of, 83–86, 88–91, 96,
  109–10, 127. *See also* phylobiological technique
tensions, physiological, 10, 74,
  83, 90–91, 96; and behavior

expressions, 84; and the eyes,
  84–90, 102, 109; sensations
  of, 49–51, 73, 103–04, 119,
  127. *See also* cotention; ditention; ocular musculature
tensions, social, 119
Thompson, Francis, 17
thought, 3, 56–57, 103, 123, 139
transference, 34, 72, 74

unconscious, the, xxxix
United Nations, 33, 43
"unity," 6 fn, 34, 38
unity, inherent, 6, 12, 17, 20, 22,
  27–28, 39, 56–57, 69, 94. *See
  also* species solidarity

war, xxx–xxxi, 16, 41–42
Western allies, 36
Wheeler, W. M., viii
*Wholeness and the Implicate
  Order* (Bohm), 12
wish, 96
world state, 146–47